TECHNOLOGICAL CHANGE
AND MANAGEMENT

The John Diebold Lectures at the Harvard Business School on the subject of "Technological Change and Management" were offered by the School in cooperation with the Department of Economics and the Program on Technology and Society, Harvard University.

TECHNOLOGICAL CHANGE AND MANAGEMENT

*The
John Diebold
Lectures
1968–1970*

David W. Ewing
Editor

HARVARD UNIVERSITY
GRADUATE SCHOOL OF BUSINESS ADMINISTRATION
Boston 1970

Distributed by
Harvard University Press
Cambridge, Massachusetts
1970

Contents

vast quantities of available information are no substitute, at the leadership level, for the ability to persuade people.

Moderator: Harvey Brooks, Dean of Engineering and Applied Physics, Harvard University

With the rise of professional managers skilled in production and marketing, the entrepreneur is becoming free of problems of efficiency and administration; he can leave them largely to the managers. This means that he can devote more time than his predecessors could to the *long-term* future, developing opportunities, social needs, and questions of *what* should be done by business and of *what* applications of technology are desirable. His role is an exciting one, and his aspirations as a businessman must be great; but he will have to meet very exacting demands from society.

Moderator: Georges Doriot, Professor of Industrial Management, Emeritus, Harvard Business School

The corporation is important not alone for the technologies, products, and services it produces, but also for the ideas, standards, and philosophies it creates. For instance, Litton and other companies have proved that there is a good alternative to the rigid, formalized chain of command that has characterized organizations since ancient times and that has usually stifled initiative and the interchange of ideas. This alternative is a looser, freer structure with a minimum of committees and conferences, and with maximum scope for individual managers to make decisions (including bad ones from time to time) and carry them out.

Moderator: W. O. Baker, Vice President—Research, Bell Telephone Laboratories

5 TECHNOLOGY AND BUSINESS OPPORTUNITY FOR THE INTERNATIONAL BUSINESS
By E. G. Woodroofe, Chairman of Unilever, Ltd.

The rise of the multinational company has enormous significance for international trade, world economic development, and more worldwide sharing of the gains of technological progress. What are the steps to becoming a mature multinational company whose management is open to the people of all countries in which it operates? What are some of the advantages and problems of mixing people of different nationalities in the same management group? How can the company make itself welcome in host countries that, while needing it, may yet fear it because of its size? Here are some answers based on the long and rich experience of Unilever's management.

Moderator: Raymond Vernon, Herbert F. Johnson Professor of International Business Management, Harvard Business School

6 NASA AS AN ADAPTIVE ORGANIZATION
By James E. Webb, Administrator of NASA, 1961–1968

Important management lessons can be learned from the experience of the National Aeronautics and Space Administration—lessons of especial value to those who would plan and lead ambitious new programs in the fields of urban development, oceanography, public transportation, health and welfare, and other areas. NASA's experience throws light on such vital questions as setting the right long-range goals, planning for changing conditions, maintaining effective control of numerous and diverse activities, developing a creative partnership with organizations in government, education, and business, and preparing for leadership succession.

Moderator: Donald K. Price, Dean, John F. Kennedy School of Government, Harvard University

Foreword

This book is a product of six John Diebold Lectures given at the Harvard Business School between November 1968 and March 1970. The lecture series was made possible by a grant from The Diebold Institute for Public Policy Studies, a non-profit foundation established in 1967 to deal with the human and social implications of scientific and technological change. The series was conceived as a means of bringing to the Harvard University community men of substantial and distinguished experience in industry and government to discuss the implications of technological change for management and society. The series was offered in cooperation with the Department of Economics at Harvard and the Program on Technology and Society.

The purpose of the lectures was expressed as follows by John Diebold in his letter of March 22, 1968 to Dean George P. Baker:

"I believe the application of science and technology to be one of the most fundamental forces of our time, changing, within our own day, not only our pace of living, our values, and the very structure of our society, but bringing about a change in man's own physical form and in the most fundamental qualities of our existence.

"Many individual responses are needed if we, as a society, are to make an informed and reasoned response to these forces and if we are to insure their use for human welfare. The lecture series that we have now established is a single step on this long road. Its objective is to bring to the Harvard community each year the men who are the leaders in bringing about this change through the application to business and to government of scientific innovations. An important purpose of the lecture series is to allow these distinguished men of administrative experience to discuss the implications for management of the complex and evolving relationships among technological change, social change, and the opportunities and challenges facing business enterprise."

Commenting on the qualities which would determine the success of the lectures, Mr. Diebold added in his letter:

"The hallmark of the series and the key to its success resides in the quality of the persons who are chosen as lecturers. They must represent a unique and rare blend of individual achievement together with the ability to contribute individual ideas and insights. The wisdom of individuals who have been able to turn ideas into reality is what we are after.

"Similarly, the choice of moderators can greatly effect the success of the lecture series. Here, I think, we are looking less for men of administrative success than for men of the most outstanding intellectual achievement.

"The second key to attaining our objectives is, I think, the care and effort exerted to plan the relationship of the individual lectures in a manner which gives a maximum of overall meaning to the series, conveying more than any one single lecture would be able to do."

The distinguished contributors to this book deal with many aspects of technological change—its past and future, its nature and dynamics, its potentials for good and evil, the opportunities and challenges it creates for business enterprise, and, in particular, its management. For just as modern management in business and government owes much of its character to trends in technology, so technology in turn is shaped importantly by management policies and decisions. Leaders and students in many fields of activity should be able to gain instruction and insight from the chapters that follow.

Many people contributed to the development of this book.

First credit must, of course, be given to John Diebold—who created, who originated the concept of the series, and whose support made both the lectures and this publication possible. My predecessor as Dean of the Harvard Business School, George P. Baker, was responsible for the role the School played throughout most of the period covered by this lecture series. Mr. James J. Foley and Mr. Edward D. Rowley, members of the School's administrative staff, together with Miss Liesa Bing of John Diebold, Inc., were responsible for the administrative arrangements involved in the lectures. Mrs. Alice McDowell prepared the manuscript for the printer, and Miss Irene Bucek handled correspondence and other duties. This volume was designed by Charles Bowker and printed by Plimpton Press. David W. Ewing, Senior Associate Editor of the *Harvard Business Review*, edited the lectures and saw the book through production.

Lawrence E. Fouraker
Dean
Harvard Business School

Soldiers Field
Boston, Massachusetts
April, 1970

1

Technology—Mainspring of History

By DONALD C. COOK
President, American Electric Power Co., Inc.

Donald C. Cook

Donald C. Cook was introduced to his audience at the Harvard Business School by Derek C. Bok, Dean of the Harvard Law School. Mr. Cook is President and Chief Executive Officer of American Electric Power Company, Inc. A native of Michigan, he has distinguished himself in the fields of government and higher education as well as industry. From 1945 to 1946 he served as executive assistant to the U.S. Attorney General, and in 1952 he served as Chairman of the Securities and Exchange Commission. He is a director of the Council for Financial Aid to Education, a member of the Board of Trustees for the Eisenhower Exchange Fellowship Program, and a member of the Visiting Committees of the business schools at Harvard, University of Michigan, and Massachusetts Institute of Technology. Articles of his on various aspects of business have appeared in *Harvard Business Review, Michigan Business Review,* and other publications. In addition to being a certified public accountant, Mr. Cook holds a master's degree in business administration and the degrees of juris doctor and master of laws.

3

P ERIODICALLY there have occurred in the history of the world certain primal events which have loosed new and pervasive forces. When they impinge on man they challenge him to appropriate response. Technology is one of these forces, and I do not believe that we can understand it or make the most of it—and of ourselves—until we understand it as a kind of mainspring of history.

In a general way we all know what the term "modern technology" means. We all have a sense of its overtones of ultra-refinement of equipment and technique coupled with massive productive power. Yet the term, in all of its implications, seems to elude precise definition. Certainly it does not include every aspect of contemporary technology. We still use hammers and wrenches, and even picks and shovels.

Neither is it limited to recent concepts or inventions. The primitive governor on a steam engine is an old instrument, yet it exemplifies the principle of feedback which is at the root of automated intra-system control.

Electric power has long been known—and even nuclear generation of it is still little more than conventional production using a different raw energy source. Yet modern technology would be unthinkable without electric energy.

Often, modern technology consists of a renascence of old discoveries through new applications arising out of urgent current needs. For example, electrostatic precipitators, now widely used for the prevention of atmospheric pollution by industry, were developed decades ago, when industrial pollution was more of a local annoyance than a national affliction.

Basic to the nature of modern technology is the accelerating effect of the breakthrough. For example, mastering the manipulation of titanium to permit utilization of its heat-resisting properties creates potentials for super-powered engines of many kinds. To see those potentials, to pursue them relentlessly, and finally to realize them creates a breakthrough. The moment we developed microwave theory and implemented it we broke through barriers in many fields of communication. Immunological techniques that make possible the transplant of one type of organ make possible the transplanting of others.

Thus each thrust through a barrier permits movement well beyond and opens the way for other significant penetrations. The result is a snowballing of development—one which in modern times can carry a single generation of men through a compressed history of technology that would have taken centuries at the older and slower paces of development.

Significant as they are, these aspects of modern technology are only peripheral. There is a strong and directed force in technological development. In part, the force is man's own perpetual search for better understanding of his world and for means to manipulate it. Man has indeed taken seriously—perhaps far too seriously—God's command to "fill the earth and subdue it." [1]

But, in somewhat the same way in which a biological organism absorbs the nutritive elements of its environment and transforms them according to its genetic pattern, technology seems to absorb human impulses and to transform and direct them. Technology impinges on its human creators and forces some kind of symbiotic relationship between them and itself.

We all recognize that life, when it first occurred on earth, was the supremely creative act of nature. And because it could generate and regenerate—life causing life—it could reach out beyond itself and create circumstances conducive to both its persistence and its destruction.

Technology seems to share some of these qualities. In a superbly creative act, man conceives and makes a wheel. The wheel cries out for an axle. The axle for a cart. The cart for a means of pulling or pushing. Soon the wheel grows teeth, engages other wheels, becomes an internal part of an engine

1. *Genesis* 1.28.

for imparting power to external wheels. These wheels need rails or roads. The whole needs sources of activating energy.

Every part of a mechanism makes insistent and rigorously logical demands for other parts of the mechanism. Every mechanism makes similar demands for others to operate in tandem with it. So, too, every process makes insistent and logical demands for evolution into less wasteful and more productive processes.

These paragenetic qualities of technology are exemplified not only in things but in concepts and ideas. The wheel and the shovel may become vastly transformed, but they never die. Addition, substraction, and the element of Euclidean geometry never die; neither does Newton's physics. All inhere, somehow, in the most sophisticated of modern formulations and concepts. Just as man is a highly refined mechanism for passing on his acculturation to generations to come, so is a power shovel or a computer an acculturated totality which will pass itself on to more sophisticated forms.

I have, of course, been describing technology in highly metaphoric terms. But no concept is formulated nor equipment built that *man* does not formulate or build. We are dealing with ideas and the physical world. Man must conceive ideas, and man must activate the physical world.

Why, then, the metaphor? Because I want to emphasize the importance of this phenomenon we are discussing—namely, the breakthrough characteristic; the acceleration of development; the umbilical connection with man's drive for understanding and mastery; the interflow of impulse between man and his technology; and—most of all—the imposition upon man of a need for very rapid, difficult, and complex adjustment. These things tell us that, in his technology, man has fashioned an element of his condition that affects and energizes him at least as much as he does it. And at times, such as now, technology seems to race forward and to leave man to tag along as best he can.

7

Elusive Challenges

Understandably, man has not been tagging along very well. For he faces the dual challenge of continuously adapting (1) his technology to suit his own nature, capacity, and desires, (2) himself and his society to meet the demands of his technology.

It is hard to say which task is the more difficult. We know, for example, that our technology is fouling our environment. But with so much of man's collective energy still bent on producing saleable goods, he has not found it easy to turn about and redivert an important part of that energy to cleaning up the environment. Although we have made some good beginnings toward a technology of environmental restoration, we need more, much more, technological development. And we need, too, an altered view and a much broader contemporary scale of burdens and benefits.

We will, I am sure, make progress in this direction. However, it is very likely that, so long as man survives, pollution will never be wholly stopped or wholly cleaned up, and, as a result, some man-made pollution may remain as a permanent part of our environment. Since an environmental condition, if it persists long enough, tends to become an evolutionary determinant, it would not be either frivolous or fantastic to suggest that we may even experience a process of ecological feedback resulting in some unforeseeable biological changes in the species.

Most of the concern about the population explosion has centered on the ability of the food supply to keep pace. However, some very credible authorities, who believe that the food supply *can* keep pace, are nevertheless very pessimistic about the consequences of population growth. Jean Mayer is one of these. His concern is the increase in people *and* in the technologically stimulated productivity of the richer nations. Al-

8

though this may sound like paradox, it becomes understandable when we consider his statement that:

"With increasing income, people stop drinking water as much; as a result we spread 48 billion (rust proof) cans and 26 billion (nondegradable) bottles over our landscape every year. We produce 800 million pounds of trash a day, a great deal of which ends up in our fields, our parks, and our forests. Only one third of the billion pounds of paper we use every year is reclaimed. Nine million cars, trucks, and buses are abandoned every year, and while many of them are used as scrap, a large though undetermined number are left to disintegrate slowly in backyards, in fields and woods, and on the sides of highways. The eight billion pounds of plastics we use every year are nondegradable materials. And many of our states are threatened with an even more pressing shortage of water, not because of an increased consumption of drinking fluid by the increasing population, but because people are getting richer and using more water for air-conditioning, swimming pools, and vastly expanded metal and chemical industries." [2]

Of course, the symbiosis of man and equipment is never perfect. Even with the best intentions it is doubtful that technology will ever produce a thoroughly safe car or that man will ever produce a thoroughly safe driver. The most convenient road for drivers may be the most destructive of landscape and environment. The best city for living and walking may be the worst for vehicular traffic. The machine that calls for a limited and highly repetitive response from its attendant may be much more efficient than one that calls for a variety of satisfying human responses. Even without the ever-present tensions and lags created by traditions and self-interest, compromises and trade-offs between inherently conflicting but nonetheless desirable social goals must always be made.

The result is that man can never wholly "find himself" in a

2. Jean Mayer, "Toward a Non-Malthusian Population Policy," *Columbia Forum*, Vol. XII, No. 2, 1969, p. 13.

technological environment. He is always needing to change the environment and, therefore, constantly challenging himself to make new adaptations.

The Struggle to Adapt

Perhaps the most troublesome aspect of symbiosis between man and his equipment has been a subtle but real change in the direction of interflow of influence. While man can still throw away a shovel or trowel that does not lie well to his hand, he is now in a culture that can—and sometimes does—throw *him* out unless he adapts to the demands of its technology.

Such adaptation may frequently be difficult—and the difficulty is not merely with people who cannot master modern physics or go into tandem with a computer. It is, in part, a difficulty inherent in the nature of man. His era of recorded history is a "blip" of time. His talents were evolved over aeons of personal confrontation with nature and materials and with the processes of his world. As a result, it is easier for him to change his implements than for his implements to change him.

Much of man's psyche and many of his talents were forged in the heat of competition and the hunt. He comes into a new world ready to fight and—by the urging of much of his nature—needing to fight. But it is a world which is less and less capable of containing conflict—whether on a two-lane road, in a crowded subway car, or in the arena of nations—without increasingly dangerous consequences. To fit himself into that world he must suppress, even if he cannot extinguish, his aggressive instincts. This suppression, however, has a cost—in feelings of inadequacy, if not guilt; in critical psychic breakdowns; and in social attitudes no longer relevant to the times.

Aggressiveness and acquisitiveness were valuable instincts in a world of scarcity. So were prudence and the habits of saving.

10

They are still valuable instincts. But the hazards and urgencies to which they were adapted are no longer quite the same in today's world. We are therefore subject to impulses and responses which are not always rational, in terms of degree or direction, for the conditions of our time.

Friendship, loyalty, even patriotism—ancient and treasured virtues—are sorely tried today, for they assume a degree of stability in one's life and one's symbols and principles, and a large capacity for personal faith. But we live in a day when life is fluid, when symbols and principles come and go, and when the whole thrust of education—in and out of schools—is to substitute inquisitiveness for faith.

Man's former closeness to the sources of his material goods was an important factor in tempering his expectations and actions. He knew his acreage and its probable yield. He knew, therefore, what were his limitations in going into debt or breeding more mouths to feed. Now, however, our technology seems to have loosed over the world an euphoria of expectations. We seem to expect an ever-increasing abundance to be able to support any level of demand we choose to impose. And this applies not only to material and financial profligacy but, beyond, to the wild extravagance with which we seem to want to destroy the values of self-restraint in every aspect of our beings.

In many ways technology magnifies the consequences of our traits and bents—and not always with happy results. In our youth the circus pitchman appeared only once a year to promise us visions of exotic beauty inside the tent. But now we are constantly showered with insistent and repetitive claims which give us fake images of what we are and what we can be if only we use Brand X. We are assaulted by the busy and incessant talk of politicians who exalt the blurred word and the unrealistic promise. All of this induces distorted images of oneself and of reality. It is not a helpful basis for understanding one's problems or for reaching sensibly toward rational solutions.

11

When acreage per person was greater than it is now, when the organic component of waste was greater than it is now, and when we bought staples in sacks and barrels rather than in cans or bottles, garbage disposal was a minor element of family life. Now it has become magnified into a national probblem. The village blacksmith could ignore the fact that his forge was belching into the air the by-products of combustion. But steel, chemical, and utility companies cannot ignore their waste products—and, incidentally, to a much greater extent than is generally realized, they do not.

The village poorhouse may have been a miserable hovel, but it could be neatly tucked away and forgotten by the community at large. Mrs. Wiggs may have lived in the Cabbage Patch, at the edge of hunger, but she was respectable and respected by the community. If you have an eye for paradox, today you may see the Cabbage Patch as a racial enclave, a backwash of the technological culture, and a focus of the welfare system which—while born out of an affirmation of humane values—is furthering the process of dehumanization begun by the technological culture.

Conflicting Environments

We have by now probed enough to begin to understand why the term "modern technology" is so difficult to define in any really adequate way, why its full implications seem to be broader than the capacity of any single mind to embrace, why thinking about it tends to set off deep feelings and disturbing questions about man's destiny, about good and evil, about vice and virtue, about social institutions and their role in man's life. These things, I believe, tell us that we are dealing with a primal force—a mainspring of human history.

Perhaps we have begun to see why it can be said that technology seems to have two environments and two modes of development. One mode is internal: a system of complex interdependencies between and among different aspects of technology. The other mode is external: a system of complex interdependencies of technology with its human creators and its human environment. And there is, of course, a wide discrepancy between these two environments—between the apparent logic and rationality of theological development and the apparent illogic and irrationality of human and social interactions with technology.

Before I go further into the problems of interadjustment between modern man and his technology, let me dwell for a moment on this contrast of apparent logic in technical and illogic in social development.

The duality is due in part to divergencies of pace. It takes an instant of history to conceive and evolve the computer. It takes aeons of evolution to bring man to the capacity for differential calculus. The duality is due in part to the different evolutionary roles of control and contingency. People do not always select their mates to produce desired characteristics in their children. And even if they were to do so, the results would be merely probable and not always foreseeable. While technology, as a human environmental factor, makes inexorable demands for rapid human adaptation, that adaptation must struggle through all kinds of ingrained tensions and impulses before it can be achieved.

The duality is, in part, an historical hangover. The first implements were doubtless created and discovered by their users. They had, therefore, an immediate and obvious relevance to those users. Invention did not become an independent engagement until late in human history. For a long time it connoted trafficking with magic or evil forces, and perhaps even trespass on the established gods—as witness the myth of Prometheus, who stole fire from the heavens and was eternally punished for it. Even as late as Goethe, a man could seriously ponder—as, indeed, Goethe did—whether the search for knowledge and power was not offensive to man's relations with God. If Goethe could ask the question, we can be sure it was an important one for his day. He was more than a poet looking at the world; he was also a scientist and philosopher.

Need for a New Discipline

But invention is no longer a questionable profession. It is an institution. It is a department of human endeavor, commanding massive endowment by both industry and government. Invention no longer is initiated merely to fill the gap between man's hand and the jobs man's hands must do. It is formulated in test tubes and computers, impelled as much by an inner routine of compulsion as by the external pressure of need. It is accomplished as much against a background of abstract scientific formulations as against a background of the visible, touchable, and immediately predictable qualities of materials and processes.

Thus invention and, as a result, technology tend more and more to generate an internal pattern and pace, independent of the pattern and pace of human and social development.

Therein, as Hamlet would say, is the "rub." Hamlet had no doubt that it was the times that were out of joint—and that it was his problem to set things right. We, however, are often provoked by the suspicion that we, and not the times, are out of joint and that the main problem is to set ourselves right.

The truth, of course, is somewhere in between. We need to develop something of the same order of skill in mastering ourselves as we have in mastering the palpable world. And we also have to perfect that mastery by a discipline which has, as its end, the service of ourselves as human beings and not the service of our machinery.

To some extent, therefore, the burden of this chapter is to illustrate the paradox. Technology has given man a greater

14

role than he ever had before in the determination of his own history. But it has set certain severe limitations on the directions he must follow. It has both widened and narrowed his alternatives. It has accelerated and intensified the rewards of intelligent response to its challenges—just as it has accelerated and intensified the penalties of stupidity and indifference.

Perhaps the first step of adaptation—technology to man and man to technology—is the development of an attitude toward both components of this duality. I wish this were easier than it actually is. A very hard lesson to learn is the difference between one's appetites and one's requirements, one's habits and one's needs, one's short-range convenience and one's long-range good.

You may well ask, "Why all this talk about duality?" After all, technology is a uniquely human product. Technological change must face very real tests before it can become part of the productive mechanism. It must solve a human problem— of thought or of action—better than a human being or an older technology can. The problem is always a practical one. We would welcome a machine that could economically clean litter off streets jammed with parked cars. But no one would have the slightest interest in a machine that could do an *entrechat* better than a live ballerina could. And, more generally, how can we in America doubt the human uses of a technology that has already contributed so much to a broader distribution of the goods of life and that promises even more?

All of this is true. But the problems which technology can solve are only those set for it. Do we always set the real problems? The most urgent ones? And, if technological America is also the most lavish material provider for its people, has it not also developed the most awesome power to kill and destroy? Is it a sign of appropriate human response that we have given over to the military our major resources and capacity for technology?

And is it a sign of appropriate human response that so much

15

human capacity is being shunted off—to the riots on and off campus, the pot parties, and the welfare rolls? Or that we have not yet achieved a goal for man except for the increased production of goods, services, and waste?

I do not think so. On the contrary, I think there is a clear need for urgent redirection of our technology—and of ourselves in the face of our technology.

I repeat, not with pessimism but with practicality, that we will never wholly succeed in these tasks. Small men and minds, big men and minds—all soon come a cropper when they come to realize the dimensions of the task; for, ultimately, the task is to make new history, impelled by a new view of ourselves, our goals, our world.

Take an obvious problem. Should every business be weighed by whether it can restore fresh air and water and livable earth as fast as it destroys them? Would you throw on the scales the social value of its product—as, for example, medical supplies? May trade-offs be made depending upon other relevant circumstances?

If you see the livable environment as a limited asset in peril of exhaustion, you may well answer "yes" to the first question and regard the others as irrelevancies. But I challenge any mind to grasp and express the full implications of this for our economic, political, social, and cultural structures.

Perhaps it is enough to say that what we want badly enough we will get—within reason. But, to begin with, we need badly a re-education of our desires. This is a small enough goal to be practical and yet large enough to be worth striving for.

Choosing New Directions

The need is not only to expand our vision but, in some ways, to narrow it. It should be clear by now that we cannot load our economy with the cost of an effective full-scale environmental clean-up on top of our already heavy national operating costs, including Viet Nam. We will have to give up something. I personally would not find it hard to give up the war, but others may have different priorities.

We may even have to give up some of our treasured liberal clichés. Our present course and rate of technological development are carrying the level of skills required in the so-called "meaningful" jobs beyond the ability of broad sections of the population to provide those skills. We are thus accentuating the distinction between the menial and the dignified job, between people in the mainstream and those merely on the fringes of it. We might even come to see that uncontrolled procreation, migration, and immigration are adding people to the fringes faster than we can direct them back.

What shall we do about this situation? To suggest forms of controls is to risk being branded a bigot, or worse. Nevertheless, the questions have to be faced.

A man steeped in the democratic tradition may soon, therefore, be agonized by a paradox. He has never before had to doubt any soul's right to be born or any human body's right to move where and how it can. But now he comes to realize that these kinds of freedom can play havoc with a society which simply cannot absorb every level of competence or every grain of impulse into its productive mainstream. At its best, such a society can only struggle to lift levels of competence and direct impulses to make them more compatible with the mainstream.

Nor is the problem solely a domestic one. Discrepancies in technological development among nations create new problems which classical diplomacy has not been able to handle. The controversy over the anti-ballistic missile reminds us again how painfully vulnerable we are, despite all our strength. We have developed—for what it is worth—the degree of restraint which comes from our vast nuclear power and the vast amount we have to lose in any contest of nuclear powers, no matter how wide our margin of superiority. But how shall we deal with an aggressor who produces a few dirty bombs and has a handkerchief of ground from which to launch them?

All of this is not to indict technology. It is merely to emphasize how difficult are the adjustments which are so badly needed.

Nor is it to suggest that technology has moral or ethical aspects. On the contrary, it is the uses to which technology is put by man that raise moral and ethical questions. The uses are but a reflection of the morals and ethics of man. In short, the human problems associated with an advanced and advancing technology arise not so much from the fact that technology pulls us whither it will but, rather, because we are not pushing it where it should go.

Perhaps this means that the period of the preeminence of science and engineering will draw to a close and be superseded by an era of dominance by the behavioral sciences—particularly sociology, economics, philosophy, and law, seasoned with a dash of anthropology and history. Perhaps the time has come for man really to know himself, and thus find himself. There is still enough time—but none too much to spare.

2

The Limits of Technology

By ELI GOLDSTON
President, Eastern Gas & Fuel Associates

Eli Goldston

Following his graduation from the Harvard Law School in 1949, Eli Goldston joined the Cleveland law firm of Hahn, Loeser, Freedheim, Dean & Wellman, and became a partner six years later. "It was a major corporate law assignment for the firm that launched Mr. Goldston on a business career," said Harvey Brooks, Dean of Engineering and Applied Physics at Harvard, in introducing the Diebold lecturer to his audience. "This was the reorganization of West Virginia Coal and Coke Corporation into Midland Enterprises Inc., whose principal operating subsidiary was The Ohio River Company of Cincinnati, one of the nation's leading river bargelines. He was president of Midland when it was acquired in 1961 by Eastern Gas and Fuel Associates. He joined Eastern as executive vice president and became president in 1962, and since 1963 has been chief executive officer and a trustee.

"In addition to his posts with the parent company, Mr. Goldston is chairman and director of 13 Eastern subsidiary companies which are engaged in the production, sale, and transportation of the raw materials of energy. Eastern's major operations are in the bituminous coal, gas utility, river and ocean barge, and marine and coke industries. He is also a director of a number of business firms, including The First National Bank of Boston, Raytheon Company, Arthur D. Little, Inc., John Hancock Mutual Life Insurance Company, and Algonquin Gas Transmission Company. He is a director of the Council on Foundations, the Boston Urban Foundation, the National Bureau of Economic Research, and the International Center of New England; and a member of the Business Leadership Advisory Council of the Office of Economic Opportunity."

21

THERE seems to be no limit to the wonders which modern technology can accomplish. Throughout the world people watch on TV as astronauts stroll on the moon. Nor does there seem to be any limit to our belief in what society can accomplish with technology. The TV camera occasionally cuts back from the moon to the pickets at Cape Kennedy with their signs, "If we can put a white man on the moon, why can't we put a black man in a decent home?" And at the Massachusetts Institute of Technology, a student group has demanded that the institution cease war and space research and instruct its laboratories quickly to solve all the problems here on earth.

Technology, after all, has made true the wildest dreams of Jules Verne and the science fiction writers. Why shouldn't it make possible the dream worlds of the Utopians? Perhaps the answer lies in distinguishing between the discovery and accumulation of scientific and technical knowledge, on the one hand, and the practical use of this knowledge, on the other hand. For many problems, we already have the necessary technology. What we lack is the ability to *implement* our knowledge. In this chapter let us examine some of the reasons for our failures to apply our technological know-how both in government and in business. Then let us look at some of the implications of this problem for management. What can management do to exploit new advances in technology? Under what limitations does it operate in trying to do this?

Sacred Cows

Perhaps the main reason for our difficulty in applying technical knowledge is that people still accept social-economic-political change slowly, yet the discovery of new technology has speeded up. Take, for example, the food problem of India.

In that nation there are about three people for every head of cattle, while in the United States there are about two people for every head of cattle. Yet Americans eat about 70 times as much meat per capita as Indians eat. Our cattle are largely raised for slaughter and serve as a major supply of food. Indian cattle are venerated as "Sacred Cows." Taking into account the grain consumed, Indian cattle actually diminish the supply of food available for humans in India.

The very simple and relatively inexpensive technology of slaughterhouses, meat storage plants, and distribution facilities would seem to be an easy way of almost instantly supplying India with a fairly generous meat supply (even by American standards). But with more than half the Indian population vegetarians, and with the protection of Sacred Cows rising almost to the level of constitutional right, no sensible person would spend much effort trying to implement this technological solution to India's food problem.

My own experience with some of the major problems in the United States has been quite comparable. There is no shortage of technology in our country, but there is a surplus of "Sacred Cows." Scientists and engineers have provided most of the technology necessary to reduce many of our social ills. But government, education, religion, business, labor—our human institutions—have habits, fears, beliefs, vested interests, and outmoded structures which are very important to them. Our human institutions struggle to protect their "Sacred Cows." Pickets at Apollo launchings at Cape Kennedy have worn signs asking why our country is better at producing space modules than at producing low-income housing. The answer, I think, is that we have not yet learned either how to use much of what we know or how to discipline technological progress as it is applied.

As a consequence, we have become uneasy about the impact of industrial technology on our physical environment, and we worry about the impact of computer technology on the humanistic quality of our life. In 1969 a panel of the National Academy of Sciences, headed by Dean Harvey Brooks, warned of the risk of grave injury to mankind from the perilous side effects of new technologies. It also pointed out that since the Federal Government pays for nearly half of the nation's research and development, it could easily have a major influence in fostering a more constructive evolution of our technological order. The panel recommended a Federal agency to assess and choose in implementing technology, and stressed that the new agency should be so designed as to be able to affect the very centers of political decision. It gives as examples of problems caused by technological changes: "the specter of thermonuclear destruction, the tensions of congested cities, the hazards of a polluted and despoiled biosphere, the expanding arsenal of techniques for the surveillance and manipulation of private thought and behavior, the alienation of those who feel excluded from power in an increasingly technical civilization."

As a business decision maker reading Deans Brooks' report, I am interested in two questions which it raises: (1) Can our environment continue to absorb the side effects of technologies which pollute water, air, and earth? (2) Can our society cope with the problems of morale and motivation which result from the affluence of a technology which is not popularly understood?

Facing Up to Pollution

Since pollution is a technological problem in the first instance, it should be susceptible to a fairly easy technological solution. Almost every engineer and scientist assures us of this.

But actually getting the problem solved is far from easy. It is a matter not of science and engineering but of cost and funding. And it isn't just a matter of the private profit system; this is important to remember because we tend too much to blame this problem on profit motives. Much of the pollution we worry about is created by government and nonprofit operations. In city after city, one of the major structures with polluting smokestacks is City Hall or a major private hospital. Amongst the defendants in any number of river and lake pollution cases are the municipalities that empty their sewage untreated into the waterways. The problem is to make a societal decision that we are ready to pay more for our electricity, pay higher municipal taxes, and shoulder the other costs of eliminating pollution.

When an organization solves its disposal problem by dumping its waste into such common property as the ambient air, it is passing on to its neighbors a part of its own operating costs. In the language of the economists, it must begin to "internalize" these costs. A power plant that spews pollution into the air is simply "externalizing" to its neighbors who suffer injury to health and property, the costs which otherwise would be internalized against its own customers or shareholders.

We certainly do not want to be the first species on earth that has made itself extinct! It took the glaciers to kill off the mastodons. It took the arrival of the white men very nearly to extinguish the American Buffalo. But there are perfectly responsible scientists who feel that we may make ourselves extinct—at least those of us who live in industrialized areas—unless we do something about applying the technology we already have to the problems of pollution we have created.

To emphasize how difficult people can find the problem of social decision, it is interesting to note that man has succeeded in destroying his environment even when he did not wield advanced technologies. For instance, in the Middle East there is a saying that "not only does the Bedouin go to the desert, but the desert comes to the Bedouin." By using a means no more sophisticated than a herd of sheep and goats, the Bedouins have, by overgrazing, returned to desert conditions a great many square miles of arable land. Similarly, the tobacco farmer of the Old South ruined his soil by overplanting tobacco. My point is that the villain is not a modern technology which can damage the quality of living. Rather, the villain is our failure to look toward the consequences of the things that we do, and our unwillingness to pay somewhat higher costs in order to prevent these consequences.

There is continuing talk about the necessity of our shifting our national priorities. I suppose that in the United States we most clearly articulate our national priorities in our federal budget. You need only look at the federal budget to see that at the present time we are prepared as a society to spend billions for military and space purposes—but not even hundreds of millions for purposes of making our environment more compatible with our lives. Historically, U.S. society repeatedly has been slow to realize a problem, and then has mounted a rapid crash program to solve it. Our real hope is that we will again make up in that way for a slow start. If we throw up our hands in dismay, we surely invite disaster. But if we press energetically for the kinds of action recommended by Dean Brooks' panel, there is abundant prospect of success.

We are already beginning to see government action and substantial efforts by numerous private firms to do something about pollution. Indeed, one of the largest growth areas in American industry is the anti-pollution field. The question is: Can we, the public, mobilize *ourselves* to meet the costs of prevention?

Man-Computer Relations

I have been discussing the impact of technology on our physical environment, that is, its external effect on human beings. But there is another equally troublesome matter: the *internal* effect on human beings. Can we cope with the problems of morale and motivation that come with high technology, particularly the effect that increased computerization of our information and control systems has on us as individual human beings?

There seems to be general discontent with the quality of the work that we offer our employees in modern factories and offices. The constant complaint on college campuses is that I.B.M., which once plastered offices with the slogan, "THINK," has now helped to produce a generation of people who feel that they have been depersonalized into key-punch cards; and in protest some students wear buttons saying, "Do not fold, spindle or mutilate. I am human." But our problem, I think, is not so much with the machinery we use as with the vast aggregations of people we assemble and organize in corporations, universities, hospitals, city agencies, and other systems for the division and control of human effort.

Professor Harry Levinson of the Harvard Business School has suggested that the complexities of people's relationships within and to organization are the central socio-psychological problems of an industrial era.[1] Tensions and alienations result not from the advent of new technology but rather from the *way it is introduced*. Let me give you an amusing example. A new computer installation gave managers direct access to the company's data base through a terminal located in their offices, with a TV-viewing screen attached. Any questions a manager might pose through his terminal were instantaneously answered; before he could take his hand off the keyboard, there was the answer displayed on his viewing screen in front of him. The human reaction was a sort of defense mechanism—to throw the computer another question. Instantaneously it would throw back the answer. Now the manager was wasting not only the computer's time but also his own time. In addition, by asking the extra questions he lost his original thought patterns, which led to further delay.

The solution to this problem was simple. The computer was

1. *The Exceptional Executive* (Cambridge, Mass., Harvard University Press, 1968), pp. 12–43.

programmed to give its answers after a ten-second delay, giving the manager time to prepare himself for the answer and conveying the additional impression that the computer had to do a little thinking itself before answering! I believe that as machinery becomes somewhat more human in its relationships with the operator, a kind of rivalry develops, a love-hate relationship between man and the machine. This was the situation dealt with by slowing down the computer's reactions. "By God," the operator said to himself then, "when I give that machine a question, it has to take time to think." When this happened, there followed a substantial reduction in the number of questions asked, and a great increase in the happiness of those people connected with the computer. The machine wasn't quite that perfect!

Nonquantifiable Decisions

Another source of tension and alienation between man and technology is our failure to recognize that many of our most important problems cannot be quantified and solved by even the most sophisticated computer techniques. After all, the computer is just a very fast but not very bright secretary. It will do very well what it is directed to do, but it cannot weigh problems of ethics, ultimate goals, and the subtleties of human relationships. Computer science can help the executive but it cannot supplant him in his most exacting decisions. People often are not creative enough to anticipate the unexpected and to devise new ways of thinking about old problems—and as for the computer, it is not creative *at all* (except to the extent that it can be loosed on, say, a random selection of new acronyms, which may *seem* to be a creative way of picking out a new name for a firm or something else, but really is just mechanical sorting).

Thus, early war game theory used by the United States in

1941 anticipated and had contingency plans for everything that the Japanese might conceivably do except what they did do—the unanticipated attack on Pearl Harbor. So the planners had to scrap all the plans and start over. Or, to take a less dramatic example, Johnson & Johnson instituted a new computerized inventory-control system based upon typical patterns of orders for its health and first-aid products. As the Johnson & Johnson managers had hoped, it turned out that the new system was so successful and so dependable that customers learned they never had to worry about Johnson & Johnson being out of stock. Accordingly, they changed their own patterns of buying and stocking inventory, and when that happened, managers at the company had to review carefully what had happened and revise their original program.

In short, even the most mathematical of business problems must be reviewed for the dynamic interplay of various factors as well as for the unanticipated result. I suppose that to the extent that some of the high-technology businesses are trying to solve purely scientific problems, such as the design of a transistor or the trajectory of a missile, there may be few unanticipatible consequences. On the other hand, no one who has ever participated in the top management decisions of a significant corporation has ever thought that management is a science rather than an art. There is some belief by outsiders and scientists that business decisions come in nicely packaged and pre-calibrated boxes so that the top manager need only read the rates of return calculated on a discounted cash flow basis; apply his average inclination or disinclination toward risk; and come out with some predictable and certain decision. But I wonder how many branch plants have been built in isolated locations where the trout fishing is good and the golf course isn't crowded, because the vice president for production fancies himself as an outdoors man? How many companies have turned down obviously more profitable new ventures because, after all, they think they know the old business?

How many top managers have taken the computer printouts and, when nobody was looking, locked the door and flipped a coin?

Experienced executives know that future events which will affect any product are not predictable within a range of 25%. Experienced executives know that the information coming to them for decision is necessarily skewed by the often unrecognized desires of the people who prepare it to favor one decision or another. Experienced executives know that the success or failure of any given project will be determined by a hundred events and decisions on down the path from the particular one at hand. We are beyond the point where our major job is to do more efficiently what we long have done. Our major job is to handle change and, fortunately or unfortunately, this is exactly what the computer can*not* be programmed to handle. As a consequence, all of the technology, all of the computer analysis, all of the vast quantity of information that can now be made available—all of these still end up subject to a human judgment. Indeed, as you move from the well-managed, scientifically managed firm (which is more the exception than the rule) toward the more personally managed or, indeed, idiosyncratically managed firm, you can discard all notions of predetermined, mathematically solved decisions.

Producing Acceptable Goals

But we must distinguish between means and ends. While recognizing the problems of management, we must consider the goals of the enterprise being managed. After all, even the humanistic psychologists who argue for new priorities and regard our present society as one of materialism and hopelessness admit that skilled managers will be needed to run their proposed humanized technology. Thus Erich Fromm wrote in *The Revolution of Hope:* "A highly complex society like that of the

31

United States, based on a large group of skilled managers and managerial bureaucracy, could not function unless equally skilled people took the place of those who run the industrial machine now. Neither the students nor the black masses offer many men with such skill. Hence, a 'victorious revolution' would simply lead to the breakdown of the industrial machine of the United States and defeat itself, even without the forces of the state, which would suppress it." [2]

The problem is not to persuade social critics that technological management has something to offer. Rather it is to recognize that our goals must be reviewed and shifted toward broad social needs. In arguing, as does John Kenneth Galbraith, for more production for public needs, Erich Fromm points out that over the past years "production and consumption have been increased, and at the same time work hours have been reduced and child labor largely abolished. This choice was not dictated by technical necessity, but was the result of changing social attitudes and political struggle. . . . In such a shift from the private to the public sector of consumption, private spending would be restrained, income would be diverted to higher taxes, and there would be a measurable shift from deadening, dehumanizing private consumption to new forms of public community activities." [3]

Where will we find the managers of technology who can meet the demands of such social critics, maintain efficiency, and accomplish their goals? We will need more than men who believe that complicated business decisions can be reduced to neat problems in pure mathematics. Matrix algebra, vector analysis, Fourier series, topology, calculus of variations, and the rest will not, as Professor Levinson suggests, "keep sight of the richness and complexity of issues." These techniques will not produce an engineering of acceptance, which is an impre-

2. Erich Fromm, *The Revolution of Hope* (New York, Bantam Books, 1968), p. 148.
3. *Ibid*, pp. 137, 139.

cise art that is increasingly needed to enlarge the limits of technology.

A good example of this, I think, can be seen in the success of James Webb, who placed a man on the moon at less cost and in less time than was promised by President John F. Kennedy. As Mr. Webb points out in Chapter 6, NASA's selection of a dramatic goal was important in coalescing support and enthusiasm among the general population, congressmen, scientists, engineers, and businessmen who had to be assembled in his project. One of the great strengths which he brought to his job was a full understanding of the idea that NASA's task was not to bring a new body of knowledge and technology into being (most of the basic knowledge and basic technology were already at hand), but to organize and manage the use of available knowledge and technology in a purposeful and effective way. This, fundamentally, was a job of organizing and managing *people*, and simultaneously making sure that citizens and their legislative representatives were in a position to understand, accept, and support what was being done.

Compare this approach with the unhappy experience of Defense Secretary Robert McNamara in his effort to achieve "commonality" in the TFX, which has become known as the F-111 and, more popularly, as the "Flying Edsel." The idea was a sensible one. There was a considerable overlap in the performance requirements of a new plane to be used by the Air Force and a new plane to be used by the Navy. It seemed that an immense amount of design engineering could be saved if a single plane could serve both purposes and that, subsequently, immense savings could be made in spare parts, maintenance, and so on. Rather than using some salesmanship and persuading the Army, Air Force, and Congress that a "superplane" could be achieved by combining all the efforts on both planes into one, McNamara emphasized the thrift that would be achieved by his so-called "cost effectiveness" concept. There probably was never a phrase that was less likely to attract a professional soldier than "cost effectiveness" or "more bang for a buck." The bitter Congressional hearings and continued dissatisfaction of the Air Force and Navy, which followed, should have come as no surprise.

In both the Webb and the McNamara programs, the technological achievement was considerable. The TFX has now been subdivided into several breeds of F-111, and each is, indeed, a very remarkable plane. But most people who have carefully studied the subject believe that even a better technological performance could have been achieved had a better job been done of persuading all of the people and interests concerned to pull together. Thus *Fortune* concludes: "It may never be possible to sort out how many of the F-111's troubles have stemmed from trying to stretch one airplane too far over the framework of commonality, how much from the military's foot dragging and 'dare-it-to-work' attitudes, which were only intensified by the Congressional hearings, and how much from problems that normally arise in any attempt to advance the state of aircraft art." [4]

A good part of many of the problems of government technology comes from a lack of salesmanship in the sense of effective persuasion (which amounts to leadership). Compare the hopelessly dragging housing programs under Housing and Urban Development Secretary Robert C. Weaver, who used such uninspiring names as "Section 221-(d)(3)" and "Section 236," with the real salesmanship of Sargent Shriver who named his programs "Headstart," "Job Corps," and "Vista." Weaver's successor, George Romney, has learned from Sargent Shriver and has named his housing program "Operation Breakthrough." What it all adds up to is that assembling technology and solving problems is primarily a question of people; of persuading workers and executives that the technology is useful and will work; and of persuading publics to support and accept it.

4. Tom Alexander, "McNamara's Expensive Economy Plane," *Fortune*, June 1967, p. 91.

Winning Over the Community

Now I want to turn to some recent experiences we have had at Eastern Gas and Fuel Associates. We have not really faced a need for a major technological advance in the eight years I have been with the company. There has been little in the way of knowledge, science, or technology that has been lacking or that has delayed anything we have wanted to do. The principal problem has been gaining the acceptance of employees, customers, neighbors, and so on—and preparing ourselves to win such acceptance.

There was, for instance, the problem we had getting approval for our subsidiary, the Boston Gas Co., to lay a natural gas pipeline through Milton, Massachusetts. Even though our plans called for using a technology that made the pipeline completely safe, and even though we offered the testimony of our own experts as well as outside consultants, the people of Milton remained opposed to the pipeline. For two years they held up the necessary permit even though the completion of the pipeline would mean better service to their own community at no cost to them (and there would be no pollution of their environment). We had hopelessly underestimated the extent to which the Negro revolution had persuaded this all-white suburb that you not only could but should "fight City Hall." Now we allow more time, more money, and more top executive attention for every right-of-way problem.

In our Boston Urban Rehabilitation Project, which has received some acclaim as BURP, we had the adequate technology for economic, rapid rehabilitation of low-income housing, yet failure to get tenant and community acceptance delayed completion and then led to rent strikes which threatened the entire urban renewal program in the Boston area. Only when we met the demands for participation by most of the black community, responding by helping an all-black team get a piece

35

of the action, was it possible for the construction to proceed in peace.

BURP had its genesis in the early fall of 1967, when the Department of Housing and Urban Development decided to conduct a large demonstration of rehabilitation in the Roxbury-Dorchester section of Boston (populated largely by blacks).

The BURP designation was originally limited to describing the allocation of $24.5 million in federal funds to five private developer-sponsors to rehabilitate 2,000 apartment units in 101 buildings. It has since been extended by common usage to cover an almost contemporaneous rent supplement program involving 731 units in 30 buildings, with an allocation of $7.5 million, and two subsequent projects sponsored by black development groups covering 217 units at a cost of $2.7 million. The central 2,000-unit award still is far and away the largest single allocation for rehabilitation the Federal Housing Administration has ever made, so it is fair to say that BURP constitutes a very significant prototype.

Our companies became involved initially because of the marketing interest of Boston Gas in the sales opportunities of such a vast rehabilitation program. (The inelegant acronym of the program name provided our subsidiary with the light-hearted slogan, "When you BURP, think gas!" We nudged a professor of city planning to challenge our electric utility competitor to come up with BELCH—Boston Edison Low-Cost Housing.) Inquiries revealed the developers' need for equity cash to make their projects go. After extensive negotiation with the developers and discussions with Federal Housing Administration officials, Eastern Gas and Fuel Associates provided this money by the purchase of equity interests in limited partnerships in a majority of the units. Boston Gas received the fuel commitment by extending its low public housing rates to the buildings, thus meeting competitive fuel costs.

Boston Gas gained its largest single addition to gas load in recent years, while Eastern received the "spillover tax shelter"

36

benefit. Neither return by itself would have justified our involvement commercially, but together the two showed a respectable profit.

BURP was successful by many standards. In 18 months, one seventh of the black population of Boston was rehoused in renovated units, with no increase in shelter cost. More than 400 black construction workers were employed at one time or another, and the majority of them were given some craft training. Two all-black development teams—contractors, lawyers, developer-sponsors, managers, and a majority of the investors— emerged to receive about 10% of the total BURP program.

As indicated, though, we had our problems. The twin goals of speed and size led to early oversights and mistakes that caused difficulties with many elements of the black community. To assemble almost 3,000 dwelling units without undue real estate speculation and complete the rehabilitation in record time, it seemed to be advisable for the FHA to move quietly in the beginning and to select established and experienced real estate and rehabilitation firms as private developers. Although the intention was good, black businessmen felt left out of the action.

Furthermore, to heighten the impact of the program, it was determined that the announcements should be made with a splash and a show. Little did we know, but danger was waiting. At the announcement luncheon, held in a black settlement house which represented the social work approach of an earlier generation, Secretary Weaver—himself a black—was interrupted and challenged by black militants as he tried to explain the program. They denounced BURP as another effort of slumlords, undertaken without consulting or considering tenants or the community, to profiteer in the ghetto.

In succeeding days an extreme cold wave, coinciding with eviction notices, brought an avalanche of public complaints of hardship. A glorious experiment appeared doomed before it started. Fortunately, we were able to counter community opposition promptly. We found that established company relationships with the NAACP, various youth and employment groups, a community social service center, and especially the widely respected black operator of a school of fine arts were invaluable resources.

Often we are visited by businessmen and others who want to know how we managed BURP and what can be learned from the experience.[5] We tell them that their principal concern, if suitable rehabilitation structures are available, should be to find the way of genuine community acceptance. To this end, they need the best possible advice from the community itself.

This means competent black advisers with whom mutual confidence has been established by previous business relationships. Sometimes they are employees, sometimes customers, sometimes community leaders whose causes the company has aided. From them it is possible to get guidance about the groups and persons who are the focal points of persuasion in the community.

It is not easy to determine the power structure or to estimate how long it may prevail. While there is a more-or-less recognized leadership, there is also, as in all other communities—but perhaps more so in the black ghettos—significant new leadership appearing within short periods of time. A company must realize that its friends of today may be the *ancien regime* of tomorrow. Plans for Columbia University's gymnasium and Governor Nelson Rockefeller's state office building originally received support from the Harlem community but were later blocked after a turnover in community leadership.

In our coal business, we were plagued with wildcat strikes during 1969 as miners pressed for greater mine safety and protection from the health hazard, "black lung," which is caused by excessive intake of coal dust over a long period of years. In

5. The most scholarly and comprehensive study of BURP is Langley Keyes, Jr., *The Boston Rehabilitation Program: An Independent Analysis* (to be published by the Harvard-M.I.T. Joint Center on Urban Studies).

response, we offered complete protection through free respirators—only to stumble against worker resistance to their use. It seemed a miner could prove his manliness by working without a respirator; also, it's difficult to wear a respirator while chewing tobacco, which is done by many miners as a compensation for not being permitted to smoke underground. When we carefully examined the technology of dust control, we found that with existing know-how we could control the dust in the atmosphere so that often the miner would not need to wear a respirator. At the same time we also did further research on the safety problem and found that other technology could be applied to prevent other health and safety hazards in the mines. But the real problem turned out to be getting the miner at the working face of the mine to perform the necessary functions and to realize the dangers created by only a partial completion of a safety routine. Despite action to upgrade our dust-control technology, and despite our expanded use of the latest developments in safety technology and our public announcement of our intentions, wildcat strikes have continued as many of the miners remain unconvinced and uncooperative. The need is for communication and persuasion.

To take a more successful example, at Boston Gas we have tried to make relationships with our customers more personalized and more pleasant. But with 300,000 customers, it became impossible to have enough clerks to keep enough records so that a customer could under all circumstances get a fairly prompt reply to a question. In our credit practices we found ourselves drifting, as have most large banks, insurance companies, and utilities, into "red lining" neighborhoods where poor people, often black people, lived. The easy procedure in these neighborhoods was to demand prompt payments and to turn the gas off promptly when payments were delinquent. However, once the computer arrived it became possible to analyze delinquencies on an almost daily basis and take into account individual credit histories. Therefore we could individualize credit warnings and gas turn-offs. We not only eliminated the offensive "red lining" procedure but actually improved our collection experience, since a good many of the deadbeats were not the poor in the central city but the affluent and often transient executives in the suburbs who had not been threatened with credit procedures merely because they lived in these favored areas. Thus we found that the automation and mechanization of operations need not produce a cold and mechanical attitude toward a company's employees and customers. And our improved collections in the suburbs more than paid for the extra cost of the computer program!

In an important new project at our barging operation, we hope to make an important breakthrough in waste disposal, one of the nation's environmental problems. We presently have a bid before one of the major river cities to compress trash and dispose of it in mined-out coal mines in another state. Interestingly enough, the technology for waste compaction, as it is called, has been available for years. For instance, reliable high-pressure presses have been in use since the baling of cotton and hay. The real problems in acceptance of our plan are (1) convincing community leaders, who fear that their political future may be in jeopardy if they back a new untried approach to their city's problem, and (2) persuading citizens in the mined-out area in another state, who fear that the compacted trash brought in will pollute their land (actually, the trash will help them reclaim it, we believe).

Conclusion

What then are the limits of technology? In short, I must fully agree with Archimedes, who said that "if you give me a place to put the fulcrum and a long enough lever, I can move the world." The *scientific* limits of technology are practically beyond imagination; what cannot be done now, with a reasonable application of science, can almost certainly be done in the future. The technical problems are just that we must consider consequences and internalize the costs.

The real limits lie in the difficulty of persuading people to give us the lever and a place to put the fulcrum—to let us feed them with the beef of their own "Sacred Cows." The persuasion is not a matter of hard sell or glossy public relations. It is a matter of empathy and leadership. Thus the limits of technology are human problems. Technology is limited not by science and mathematics and engineering, but by our ability to understand the problems of our society and to assemble the necessary public support behind workable solutions.

3

The New Entrepreneur

By JOSEPH C. WILSON
Chairman of the Board, Xerox Corporation

Joseph C. Wilson

Joseph C. Wilson joined The Haloid Company in Rochester in 1933, and became its chief executive officer in 1946. In 1961 the company's name was changed to Xerox Corporation. Since 1966 he has been Chairman of the Board; he is also co-Chairman of Rank-Xerox, Ltd., in London. In addition to serving as a director of a number of other companies, he has been active as a trustee of various organizations, including the National Conference of Christians and Jews.

He was introduced as a Diebold lecturer by General Georges Doriot, who had taught for many years at the Harvard Business School. "Your speaker is an able businessman—a public-spirited citizen who transformed a medium-sized company into a large, very successful one," Doriot said. "In 1953, sales were $15 million. In 1958, sales were $27 million. In 1967, sales were $701 million, obtained mostly through internal growth. [Xerox's annual sales are now past the $1 billion mark.] You might say that his story is a tale of three cities:

"An inventor in New York City;

"A research institution in Columbus, Ohio;

"A fairly indifferent company in Rochester—as a base.

"Then a man came and did what we should all do many times while we live. He gave the spark of life to men and ideas. The result is Xerox of today. We admire and wish to learn from him."

THE entrepreneur of today has a more complicated job than the entrepreneur of yesterday had—a job with added dimensions and intellectual challenge. The entrepreneur of tomorrow will have a more exacting role still. Of course, technological change is one of the reasons for this trend.

At the same time, the task of the entrepreneur is becoming one that he finds more satisfying; there is more emphasis on objectives now and less on administration. Moreover, the opportunities for entrepreneurs are great—in some respects, greater than they ever were. And their role in society has become more significant; without them, the potential benefits of technology would be mostly lost. Paradoxically however, it seems likely that unless entrepreneurs today and tomorrow do their jobs well, they will be downgraded in our society.

These are some of the beliefs I wish to develop in this chapter.

Traditional Qualities

In some respects, the new entrepreneur is the same man he always was—innovative, daring, determined, different from most people. Stripped down to his essentials, he is rather like a highly sophisticated Tom Swift, who is now a very "in" hero after many decades of obscurity. You may recall Swift as a daring young man of infinite imagination, industry, and bravery, who brooked no obstacle in the headlong drive to succeed.

In nearly all of the literature on the subject, certain key adjectives and concepts recur in the description of the entrepreneur and his role. For instance, witness what Dr. Michael Young had to say about the enterpriser in his *Rise of the Meritocracy:*

"Civilization does not depend on the solid mass, but upon

the creative minority, the innovator, who, with one stroke, can save the labor of ten thousand, the brilliant few, who cannot look without wonder, the restless elite who have made mutation a social as well as a biological fact. Progress is their triumph, the modern world their monument." [1]

William Miller elaborates on the idea in his introduction to a book of essays on the entrepreneur's historical role, entitled *Men in Business*. He says:

"Entrepreneurship, by its nature, abhors channels. In the past, as these essays show, it has tended to be individualistic, innovative, venturesome." [2]

The entrepreneur may be defined somewhat less colorfully as one who assumes both the risk and the management of an enterprise, and who hires managers, provides guidelines for their functions, and performs within the organization. He is a man who has ideas—basic, germinal ideas, not vagrant thoughts —and who has the daring and the confidence to use them. He is the leader of people who will become leaders. He is the manager who steps out beyond the confines of a specific area of corporate responsibility. He creates, he pioneers, not just to be different, but simply because *this sort of activity expresses his whole being.* Decades ago Henry Ford innovated on what was then a stunning scale when he instituted the $5 a day minimum wage. Joseph Lincoln took the same sort of giant step when he devised and inaugurated his famous profit-sharing plan at Lincoln Electric Company. Both were entrepreneurs in every sense of the word. The public may know them only for their companies and products, but they pioneered in the ways just mentioned as well as others.

I shall not try to call the roll of men like this—their number is legion—but they are a very, very small perceatage of the populace. All were creative in one way or another, even in-

1. New York, Random House, 1959; p. 12.
2. Cambridge, Harvard University Press, 1952; p. 5.

ventive. Their use of creative management devices has put the tatoo of "entrepreneur" on them for all time.

Of course, the innovative spirit is a very personal thing, not easily brought out in a large organization. Yet many of us in business are anxious to encourage it. What can we do? The intangible supports are more important than any of the specific ones. What we try to do at Xerox—and I'm afraid it's faltering in many cases and does not always succeed—is to try to get our younger people to feel that the ones who are willing to accept risks (and who therefore are going to make some mistakes and have some failures) are going to progress much more rapidly with us than the ones who play everything safe and close to the chest, and who never get into trouble. It takes a very, very long time, I think, for this kind of attitude to seep through an organization of several thousand people, but I think that can happen if there is enough sustained management support.

Evolution of a New Dimension

The qualities just mentioned have always characterized the entrepreneur. What has happened to produce a change in his attitude and philosophy—in particular, to broaden his thinking about his role in life? To explain, we must take a brief look back into history.

Entrepreneurs have usually been thought of as men of commerce and business. Consequently, throughout history they have tended to share the stigma which has been persistently attached to business. In its finer moments business has been considered only as amoral, rather than immoral. Plato considered the very nature of business demeaning to the spirit. Even St. Thomas Aquinas had to back into a negative defense of the profit motive with the comment that "there is no reason why gain may not be directed to some necessary or honorable end."

49

The industrial revolution sired the embryo of the industrial society we know today. The hard-core cadre of this revolution —the early entrepreneurs—addressed themselves primarily to seeking out the most efficient ways to produce and market goods and services. During the first phase, at least, their prime areas of concern lay in design, production, and sales, all, of course, in quest of profit. They did not have to wrestle with problems of technological acceleration, of heavy forward commitment of capital resources, of management development. Their concern for people was often minimal, except to the extent that people were essential tools in the process and thus had to be cared for to some extent. Even so, people were the cheapest and most expendable of all the tools employed.

As usually happens with revolutions, the results were seldom tidy and not essentially noble. But in time there began to emerge a more enlightened self-interest on the part of some business people. These men came to perceive the benefits implicit in more humane treatment of people. They viewed employees as productive fellow humans who constituted part of a market, not merely tools. This view was, perhaps, largely based on pragmatic self-interest, yet it marked what was, with apologies to Mao Tse-Tung, "a great leap forward." It was phase two of the revolution. Significantly, this period also saw the rise of unions.

In my view the onset of World War II catapulted us into phase three of the industrial revolution. The United States' entry into the war, and its role as "the arsenal of democracy," created a demand for efficient industrial production on a scale that man had never before witnessed, perhaps never even contemplated. From "Rosie the Riveter" to instant liberty ships by the gross, this nation called upon every resource in the war effort. This was responsible for a remarkable expansion of the technological skills of management that so distinctly stamp our present society.

The vastly enhanced demand for trained managers and

skilled leaders following World War II was evident in the mushrooming of schools of industrial management. Along with, and maybe because of, the proliferation of such schools, there arose what we know now as scientific management. (There is, I realize, a sharp division of opinion as to whether management is, or ever can be, a true science, and I shall try to beware of that swampland of semantics.)

I submit that schools of management could not have come to play their critically important roles in meeting industry's demands for leaders unless management had become endowed with at least *some* of the hallmarks of a science, or at least of a profession. Whatever the difference of opinion on this, there are few students of the subject today who would deny that the management process has become relatively stable. I do not mean to imply a static process nor to indicate that the problems of management have become less complex (on the contrary, just the opposite has happened), but rather to suggest that we have developed a much better understanding of the techniques and approaches to use in tackling the problems of running an organization.

The functions of management have become reasonably well formalized. They tend to follow a common pattern throughout industry, without significant variations between major companies. Having come to a better understanding of modern management, we can not only develop and nurture them but also, to a degree, integrate backwards, as it were, and inculcate them. We must not make the mistake of minimizing the need for sustained effort toward a better understanding and refined improvement of the techniques. But our prime problems today, it seems to me, lie less in the sphere of how to do it and considerably more in *what* to do. This is the most important point to understand.

Social Awareness and Responsibility

The connotations of industrial management's arrival at a state of relative stability are more significant than may appear at first. The entrepreneur no longer has to devote himself solely to the problems of manufacturing and selling. He is free to dedicate more of his time and effort to thinking about the longer term future, to planning, to analysis of the probable environment X years hence, with all its opportunities and all its perils. This is one of several factors that have contributed to making industry, along with government, the ultimate source of power in many countries, our own included.

Confident that their organizations possess sufficient operating know-how, entrepreneurs can devote an increasing amount of their intellectual energy to devising new means of coping with the almost unbelievable complexity that emerges from any perceptive analysis of the future. Happily, this is precisely the sort of projective thinking that appeals most to entrepreneurs. It must be added, though, that the exciting opportunities they discern through the mist are accompanied by problems which are almost frightening in their dimension and nature.

I shall not dwell on the technological explosion with which the entrepreneurs of tomorrow will have to cope. John Diebold summed it up when he stated:

"Today's crops of machines deal with the very core of human society, with information, its communication and use. These are developments that offer far more to mankind than net changes in manpower, more or less employment or new ways of doing old tasks. This is a technology which vastly extends the range of human capability, and which will fundamentally alter human society, and force us to reconsider our whole approach towards society and to life itself." [3]

The question to be raised here has to do with the implications of such an age for business leaders. How will they think

3. Address to Columbia University, Alumni Day, June 3, 1963.

about their roles in society? Peering into the near future, Robert Heilbronner has this to say:

"There are, it seems to me, important possibilities for social evolution still unexplored within the business system . . . and, I hope, that in the hands of that new guard uncommitted to the ideological fundamentalism of the old guard, liberal capitalism might develop with greater stability, less poverty, more public concern." [4]

Many of us in business, I think, have come to the view that industry must explore these possibilities for social evolution. The late Gerald Phillipe, the chairman of General Electric, said to the National Association of Manufacturers:

"Our ultimate goal must be something better than merely reducing the unemployment rate, even something better than full employment opportunity for minority groups." [5]

As many Negroes are pointing out, in this country we had full employment on the plantations over a century ago.

In no other society has the businessman been accorded the standing and prestige that he has in America, and if we businessmen are not going to take a major role in tackling and eventually solving the problems in our cities, then who will?

Elisha Gray, the chairman of Whirlpool Corporation, said it more succinctly: "If not us, who? If not now, when?"

Now, I want to go further than calling simply for "good works" by management. Business students (among others) must surely have developed something of a guinea pig complex as a result of serving as a captive audience for preachers of what is loosely called "the corporate philosophy." The theme of self-redemption through good works has been so belabored that it is in danger of becoming a dead horse. Social irresponsibility, on the part of corporations, is now anachronistic.

Whatever the motivation—fear of not-so-bloodless revolu-

4. "The Power of Big Business," *Atlantic Monthly*, September 1965, p. 93.
5. Address delivered in December, 1967.

tions, enlightened self-interest, changing times, sense of duty, or something else—the corporate sense of social responsibility has become a reality in our country. Business leaders know it is essential to any corporation that wants to survive and thrive and prosper. They need to recruit and retain in their companies the most highly talented young people; and the best young people now, in my considered opinion, insist that life and work must be meaningful and must have worthwhile social goals.

Accountability for Social Results

The requirement, as I see it, is for more than responsibility in the usual sense. Because business policies and principles, as Peter Drucker once noted, "determine, very largely, the character of our society," corporate entrepreneurs are going to be held accountable in large part for the total performance of society, for the quality of life in our country and perhaps in the world. If we fail to achieve social progress quickly enough and on a broad enough scale, leadership will fall to other segments of society which will seek their own solutions—and some of these solutions would violate everything we businessmen believe in as being best for people in the long run. I believe that society is rapidly reaching a point where, if solutions (or the reasonable hope of them) are not foreseeable, the institutions which are now in existence, particularly private enterprise, will probably have their role downgraded. As for what will emerge in terms of additional controls by the government, or a rightist movement, or something else, I am not wise enough to forecast.

Thus today's entrepreneurs are compelled to concern themselves with *creating* and maintaining the sort of world in which we want to live. But, I have been asked, is not such a role incompatible with the entrepreneur's outlook? Is he not a zealot who is usually at odds with society instead of concerned about it? I do not see him in this manner. Granted, there seem to have been a good many cases of that kind, judging from reports. But I know of just as many cases on the other side. For example, the man who invented the process which has been the source of Xerox's growth was a zealot, and he worked all by himself to do it, in a kitchen. But he is the most socially minded person I have ever met. It is true that he is able to do more for community causes, now that he has quite a chunk of our company's stock, than he could when he was working as a patent attorney in New York during the depression and getting $30 a week. But I know for a fact that his spirit has remained the same throughout his life.

The Socially Useful Profit

As the locus of responsibility for most of our country's productivity, industry is a fundamental source of power for good or evil. It is instrumental in effecting many of the changes that occur in our society. What about the profit motive then? Is it consistent with the realities of business power?

Many people are familiar with the concept of the quality of a company's earnings: they knew that sophisticated analysts put as much stress on the composition and character of an organization's profits as on the dollar amount of its profits. I suggest that the socially useful profit is becoming increasingly important. I refer to the cultural and spiritual profit that accrues to the national community and to the entire society as a result of healthy economic profit. Dollars and cents are not the only end result of business effort; in a way, in fact, they are only the beginning, the fuel that keeps the system operating. This system, in turn, merits survival only if it benefits everyone along the line.

Let me offer an example that is of especial interest to our management group at Xerox. Industry produces the sustenance required to nurture and extend our system of education, and it creates the major demands for the products of that system. Indeed, many of us in industry believe that education is the greatest, most promising single field of endeavor and the best hope for solutions of the terribly complex problems with which our country is beset.

It is also the world of education that will soon constitute a vast market for a variety of goods and services, many of them still undreamed of. The $4 billion we spent on it annually at the end of World War II has grown to $50 billion, an annual rate of increase of more than 12%. Serving this market offers what some of us choose to think of as a socially useful profit.

But success in such an endeavor depends on the manner of approach. An article in the *Saturday Review* by Wilbur Ferry, Vice-President of the Fund of the Republic, carried an alarming title, "Must We Rewrite the Constitution to Control Technology?" Mr. Ferry was not being flip in his choice of this title; he rested it on the thesis of what he calls "growing evidence that technology is subtracting as much or more from the sum of human welfare as it is adding." [6] And when he wrote of the rapid growth of education as a market, it was to charge that the object was profits, not education. Of course, I disagree with the implication of his charge. But I cite this voice of dissent as a reminder that technology itself is blind, that it serves man for good only to the degree that those who direct it are first interested in bettering the human condition, and *then* in profits.

There has always been a ready, understandable tendency to fear technological change for the very reason that it is blind. What some of us view as a means for the advancement and emancipation of man is a Frankenstein to others. If it is true that business must become increasingly technology-oriented (simply because technology is one of the overriding facts of our lives), then it is also true that business, in general, must become progressively more oriented to social problems. Tech-

6. March 2, 1968, p. 50.

nologically strong companies, above all, should relate closely to society because they are becoming a prime force in its direction and development.

Additionally, businessmen, like our founding fathers, have a decent respect for the opinion of mankind, and mankind is insisting that every institution prove its social utility. A large part of my own optimism for the creative, humanistic utilization of technology derives from the fact that increasing numbers of companies are assigning corporate, not just personal, responsibility for awareness of and orientation to the issues and problems with which our world and our society are faced. It is my own conviction that great rewards—generally, in fact, the greatest—tend to come to those entrepreneurs who can perceive human needs that others have not detected or identified, and who possess the innovative talent for creating goods and services to meet those needs.

Looking Ahead

As the world grows increasingly complicated, so will the demands on entrepreneurs. Therefore we must have larger numbers of men who truly understand the nature of their industrial environment and have the courage to act in that light. Ideas alone are not enough. Those who have them must know what to do with them, and how to translate them into reality.

I have been asked on occasions if this is a practical possibility in view of what John Kenneth Galbraith calls the "technostructure" of most modern large corporations.[7] Can socially minded leaders hold sway when they must rely heavily on large numbers of experts? I am all too aware of the problem—I cannot hope to keep up with the scientists we work with at Xerox. I have to rely often on their judgment. Yet they in turn are influenced a great deal, I think, by executives who possess the

7. See *The New Industrial State* (Boston, Houghton Mifflin, 1968).

kind of philosophy I have described. Also, we in general management have the power of selection. At our company, for example, we try to bring in the kinds of experts who are conscious of social needs. While we are not in full control of events, therefore, we are better able to influence them.

Now, the approach to business leadership just described is not without its critics, including some within the business community—and surely this will continue to be the case. I recall a somewhat unsettling article in the *Wall Street Journal* which dealt with whether major corporate executives were spending too much of their time on community activities, on good works, if you will. The article pointed out that these executives were, in the last analysis, being paid to take care of the business. Yet this is exactly the point I am making: business leadership *must* involve itself in activities and problems of the broader community *as part of the job* of taking care of business. Almost as important as good corporate citizenship is the articulation of why businessmen are concerned and committed. Throughout history their motives have always been subject to scrutiny, doubt, and skepticism—and quite properly, I guess. We therefore have to be able to expound long-term objectives and their implications, which increases the need for leaders to think beyond the perimeters of their own industries. We have reached a point in time when a business leader must feel comfortable in the world of ideas.

"What about your shareholders?" people sometimes ask. "How do they feel about using their funds for social purposes?" At Xerox, to take a case in point, I suppose that the shareholders do not agree with many things we do. But, unfortunately, there is no way of consulting with all 100,000 of them about every activity we take up, whether it happens to be a research project, an effort to diversify, an acquisition, or an effort to engage in certain social activities. They have entrusted us with a certain amount of power to carry out certain of our decisions, and if they rebel against us because we go too far astray, they will throw us out. During the past few years some shareholders whom I choose to think of as narrow-minded, have tried to put resolutions before the annual meeting to the effect that we should stop doing some of these things such as supporting higher education. In the meetings these resolutions were overwhelmingly defeated. As a matter of fact, the more votes we took, the smaller the vote in favor of the opposition. So I think shareholders, broadly, are beginning to understand that the total environment is important to Xerox (or any other business). Those who disagree can exercise a well-known freedom that all stockholders have in this nation, the freedom to sell.

I hope that stockholders around the nation will join increasingly with business leaders in a very important test of social responsibility: helping the so-called "unemployables" in minority groups. In Rochester, about 50 large and small companies committed themselves to take certain "hard-core" people, employ them even if completely unqualified by normal standards, and try, at corporate expense, to train them and get them to work. They did this before the National Alliance of Businessmen asked them to do so; in fact, the NAB program imitated aspects of the Rochester companies' program. We also joined to create businesses located in or near the inner-city areas, where the difficulties were. In this effort there was a great deal of cooperation between members of the non-white groups there and managers of such companies as Xerox. In addition, 30 or 40 small and large companies in Rochester began trying to find ways to break some of the bottlenecks of low-income and middle-income housing that were afflicting the community.

This is the kind of cooperative spirit that is so important. It goes beyond making a business out of every activity—there is no profit in the projects just mentioned, though there is expense. Such activities are an investment in the future of our society. They need to be done in 150 large cities in the United States.

To sum up, an understanding of society is very important to the entrepreneur of today. It will be even more important for the next generation of business leaders. Moreover, I predict that the truly critical moments for decisive and constructive leadership will come during the next generation. We can see them coming now, though their exact shape and form are not clear yet. Clearly, the entrepreneurs of the next generation will have to be broader gauged and wiser than their predecessors in my generation have been, if they are to play a decisive part in developing a greater society in our country and in the world. I think the alternative is their elimination. Their aspirations must be higher than ours are. Their goals must be more deeply challenging. They must better understand words like these of Robert Browning's:

> That low man seeks a little thing to do,
>   Sees it and does it;
> This high man, with a great thing to pursue,
>   Dies ere he knows it.
> That low man goes on adding one to one,
>   His hundred's soon hit;
> This high man, aiming at a million,
>   Misses an unit.[8]

8. "Bells and Pomegranates—A Grammarian's Funeral."

4
The Role of Modern Business

By CHARLES B. THORNTON
Chairman of the Board, Litton Industries, Inc.

Charles B. Thornton

Charles B. Thornton is Chairman of the Board of Litton Industries, Inc. He was introduced to students at the Harvard Business School by W. O. Baker, Vice President—Research at Bell Telephone Laboratories. "Mr. Thornton," said Mr. Baker, "is the exact contradiction of my own version of the French comment on the life of mankind which says: 'He was born a man but died a manager.' He was born not in a town or village but in a county, Knox County of Texas, a dimension which well suits his subsequent endeavors and activities. He studied business early—at George Washington University. He has received from George Washington, and from other institutions, later recognition of his role. He has also exercised in business, in notable ventures like the Ford Motor Company, the Hughes Aircraft Company, and others, both direct responsibility and indirect responsibility as a director or general counselor. But even before— and always since—his interest was attracted to the endeavor known as Litton Industries.

"He has contributed also to the national security and well being, not only through his distinguished record in the last World War, with decorations of very great importance, but in addition as a consultant to the Defense Department, to the Air Force, and to various other ingredients of our defense establishment, including the present Defense Industry Advisory Council.

"Mr. Thornton has combined this experience with a great and persistent interest in economic well-being in the nation. In 1968 he received the Business Leadership Award of the University of Michigan; in 1967 the Business Leadership Award of the University of Southern California; and in other years, other rewards."

As a businessman and industrialist, I work with scientists, engineers, and technical people, among others. Not too many years ago, very few scientists wanted to be identified with business. Recently I was talking with a friend, a scientist, who had founded a very successful technological company some twenty-five years ago. He was telling me how he got started and mentioned that he had avoided linking his name to the company during its earliest stages. I asked why. He explained that he was a chemistry professor at one of our leading institutions at the time, and that he had decided to organize a small company on the side in order to exploit a technical product he had conceived. "But I didn't want my name associated with it," he told me. "I wanted to conceal the fact that I owned the company or even had an interest in it. I felt I would be inviting the ridicule of other scientists and engineers in the academic community."

This may sound like a story out of the nineteenth century, but it happened near the end of World War II. Of course, things have changed since then; today business and industry are held in higher esteem by scientists, engineers, and most of the institutional academicians. Yet we in business are still disturbed by the criticisms that are directed against our "establishment" by some segments of the public and members of government.

I believe that one of our problems in business is that we do not speak up enough. We are not getting across the message of what we are doing. We are contributing important products and services—that much is well publicized. Not so well known but equally important (and perhaps more important in the long run) are the ideas, methods, standards, and philosophies we develop for society. In this chapter I shall take one company as a kind of "case example" and examine some of its actions and thinking. That company is the one I know best—

Litton Industries. Particular attention will be paid in these pages to Litton's contribution to ideas about organization, for this work has been especially important to me and it is relevant to many important interests and aspirations of Americans.

The Corporate Setting

Since Litton Industries is often referred to as a technologically oriented company, let me begin with a few background notes on the corporate setting.

It is said that during the last twenty years there has been a doubling of the world's scientific and technological knowledge accumulated since the beginning of recorded history. Many people believe, and I agree, that such knowledge will double again in the next ten years. It is also said that 90% of all the scientists and engineers who ever lived are alive today.

Furthermore, as late as 1940, only $345 million was spent annually on scientific research in the United States. In contrast, the best estimate for 1968 is something over $20 billion. Even taking inflation into account, that is a substantial increase. To that amount we should add the cost of development, engineering, design, and production to arrive at the full measure of our scientific and technologically based effort.

Although research is carried on by colleges, universities, and government laboratories as well as by business and industry, it is the responsibility of private enterprise to develop the resulting knowledge and technology into useful products. Companies are the only elements of society charged with building, manufacturing, marketing, and distributing new products.

Through business and industry, as we all know, the advance of science and technology has yielded a tremendous flow of new products—products that never existed before, plus hundreds of thousands of others that have been redesigned, incorporating either in whole or in part some new science or technology. These products have given us better health, better food, better clothing, better shelter, and a higher standard of living.

So far this is a familiar story. What about industry's contribution to the world of ideas and philosophies? At the same time that it has been pioneering with new products it has also been bringing about many new management techniques and innovative concepts. This does not mean that older management methods have become obsolete, but that it is becoming more important to recognize which of the older techniques, policies, and methods are still valid, which need to be refreshed, remodified, and reapplied, and which should be discarded completely. This brings us to the experience of Litton Industries.

We started out as—and continue to be—a technologically based, technologically oriented company. We have more than 105,000 employees, of whom more than 10,000 are scientists, engineers, and technicians. We produce more than 9,000 different products in 227 principal plants in the United States and 16 foreign countries, and we sell these products in more than 95 countries of the free world. Of our almost $2 billion worth of products sold annually, approximately half incorporate, either in whole or in part, new technology developed within the last five years. The remainder of our products incorporate new technology developed within the last ten years.

Decline of the Rigid Organization

Now, in managing a rapidly changing company of this kind, you cannot rely upon the status quo. You must have a developing, progressing, viable organization. Because of that fact, I am asked frequently how one organizes a technologically based company. This is a controversial question, and you can get as many opinions on the subject as you can on politics or religion.

At the outset, let me say that I am a strong proponent of or-

67

ganization—of the form that creates a dynamic environment within which specific goals can be achieved through the cooperative efforts of people. This means variety and experimentation—more than leaders ever advocated before in the history of human institutions. I believe that there are many acceptable ways to organize an activity, be it a profit-making business, a government agency, or an institution. The purposes for which organizations exist, the environments in which they operate, the character of their activities, and the availability of managerial skills vary so greatly that there is no standard, optimum way of approaching the problem.

I know that some older, established, and successful companies—which are at least partly in the mainstream of new technology—use a formalized, standardized type of organization. The assignments and responsibilities of each executive, each supervisor, and numerous other individuals are defined in minute detail. Numerous committees meet frequently and render decisions which are documented and distributed throughout the organization by written directive or issued in voluminous policy and procedural manuals. Directives are handed down from manager to manager, and from manager to submanager, usually in the form of written memoranda which insure that proper procedure has been followed. Sometimes the recipient of a memo occupies an office right next door to the sender.

Although some executives and managers in business and in government agencies prefer this type of organization, and although it may be satisfactory for some activities, I feel it is rather like walking in a cemetery at dusk, laboriously reading headstones. If I were to install this kind of organization at Litton Industries, I am certain that all of our principal executives would resign, including the chairman of the board.

The rigid, formalized organizational structure has dominated the scene since ancient times. Judging from what many young people, writers, and other observers say, it is still seen as the pattern in the various "establishments" of today. Yet the *fact* is that it is rapidly becoming obsolete—at least, in a growing sector of the business world. I do not say all of the business world because I recognize that many companies, including small ones, still depend on the traditional, rigid form—or try to. A few years ago the president of a small industrial company, having less than 1,000 employees and sales just over $15 million per year, was enthusiastically extolling the future of his company. He displayed charts showing how sales and profits were going to increase. When asked why he was so confident he would accomplish this growth, he said it was because he had organized his company in such detail that it would operate automatically, and that he had volumes of manuals and organization charts to prove it. Needless to say, that company no longer exists. Its former president, as you might expect, is now a most successful organizational consultant!

As indicated earlier, I am not opposed to organization structure per se. I believe in it and recognize the need for it. And I certainly do not advocate the other extreme—a near or total absence of organization. But I do feel it is possible to over-organize a company or an activity. For some people organization often becomes an end in itself, and this tends to create a Parkinsonian kind of problem, leading to situations wherein a company's real objectives are obscured by excessive preoccupation with organizational detail or by the pursuit of organizational perfection, which of course is unattainable.

The formal, highly detailed organization of a company is not a guarantee of effective management, sound planning, or profitable operations. Instead, it usually produces a static, impersonal, and inflexible structure, with artificial barriers erected between each executive and each echelon. Effective communication and the interchange of ideas are restricted if they exist at all. Initiative and the urge to create and to change are stifled by the extreme insularity and by the sluggishness—in some cases the immovability—of a cumbersome and intractable mass.

69

If this is the image of organization possessed by the youngsters, novelists, teachers, and others who castigate business, I do not blame them. We in business leadership had better blame ourselves for a poor job of communications.

The Straight-line Approach

The best type of business organization, in my opinion, is that which strikes a balance between the formalized, tightly controlled company and the loosely controlled, free-wheeling company in which only a few people have a clear idea of where it is headed.

I can best illustrate my point by describing how Litton Industries is organized. In the first place, except for legal and accounting matters, we try to keep manuals, procedures, and administrative policies at a minimum. We have organizational charts, but they are guides; there is nothing "holy" about them. Constant communication between our executives is maintained either by telephone or preferably by personal visit. We strive to create an organizational climate in which individuals at all management levels are encouraged to exercise their full capabilities. This environment provides ample incentive and opportunity for an executive to achieve his personal fulfillment, and yet enables the organization to maintain that delicate balance between adequate control and chaos.

We have no committees. Instead, we assign responsibility to each executive—plus authority commensurate with that responsibility.

In years past I was an executive of an operating division in another company. I had a substantial amount of responsibility but little or no authority; the latter was retained by people who were not only located in a remote corporate headquarters, but also had little or no understanding of the type of business in which the division was engaged. It became all to clear to me that responsibility without authority made a management job much more difficult, if not impossible, to accomplish. I decided that if I were ever in a position to determine how a company was to be managed, I would make it a cardinal rule that responsibility would always be accompanied by commensurate authority.

While we have no committees at Litton, we do have many conferences. But there is no fixed, predetermined roster of attendees. If a certain subject is being discussed, the only people we bring into the meeting are those who can make a contribution to the issue at hand. We do not bring the public relations man in when we are talking about an engineering problem. We do not bring the accountant in on a legal problem. And we do not bring the lawyers in on a production problem. For when all members of a fixed-membership committee come to a meeting, those who know the least about the subject are too often compelled to speak up to justify their presence and their membership.

We take no votes in our conferences because the man in charge of a meeting has the primary responsibility for resolving, implementing, or carrying out the issue under consideration. He makes the decision. He may not make it at the meeting, but when he leaves he knows he has one to make.

Is this too harsh and Spartanistic a way to treat executives? Some people have told me they think so. But we do not want our executives hiding behind a committee. The fact that committee work frequently yields poor results is only part of the problem; there is also the time delay and the procedural delay. It takes much longer for a committee to function than for what I call a "straight-line" organization to function.

People have asked whether our philosophy leads to more errors and to more bad decisions. This is difficult to answer. I know of no way to tabulate whether you make more bad decisions without committees than with them. But I am certain that without committees the whole company moves faster, and one can get the job done with much more facility and dispatch. The company also has a different atmosphere. It has spirit. Morale is higher.

Leaders Who Succeed or Fail

Should a man be severely penalized when he makes a bad mistake or a bad decision? My answer is no. What counts most is his batting average. If he is right nine times out of ten, he is first-rate. Don't condemn him for the one mistake; give him credit for the nine wise decisions. Try to help him so that he may avoid making that bad tenth decision again—or one like it.

Litton executives do not have employment contracts. If an executive can assume responsibility and can effectively produce, it is not necessary to give him a contract. I do not believe in five,- ten-, or twenty-year employment contracts for executives, regardless of whether or not they meet the requirements of their positions. In lieu of contracts, our executives are treated as mature and responsible leaders and as organizers of both human and material resources. And they are well compensated.

If an individual wants employment security at Litton Industries—and I think a similar policy might well apply to many other companies—he should not seek a position in the executive group; he should stay at lower levels of the company, or drop down where there is less responsibility, more directed work, and, of course, less authority.

We think of an executive as a leader who either succeeds or fails. This may sound impersonal but that is not the way it works. Rather, we have found it a warm, stimulating kind of relationship.

How do we pick executives? We observe how a man assumes responsibility, how he works with other people, how visionary he is, and how well he can accomplish a complex management job. We have found invariably that an executive who picks

72

weak subordinates is himself a poor executive. He is unsure of himself. He is fearful that a strong subordinate will make him look bad or give him competition.

We try to avoid the executive who "knows all the answers." In the complexities of modern business and industry, such a man is not smart enough to know what he doesn't know, and his decisions will frequently create problems. The days are long past when the "industrial tycoon" can master any job in his company. I am referring, of course, to the complex, broadly based, technologically oriented industrial company. In some smaller and more simplified companies the old methods may still apply.

Decisions in Developing People

We are often asked about the turnover of executives at Litton. Do they progress? Do they leave? Can we demote them? Can we motivate them? Let me cite our experience.

In the first place, we have several hundred executives in what we call the key management group, ranging in age from thirty-five to fifty-six (the average age is about forty-two). A man in this group can look forward to two things. Of course, the first is that some day he may become president or chairman of the board of Litton Industries. We don't discourage that ambition; we like it. The other thing is a building up of the areas of activity for which he is responsible. The managers are dedicated to that objective. And instead of knowing all the answers, they welcome all the advice they can get—not only from subordinates but also from any other part of the organization, including, of course, the corporate group.

Occasionally an executive may not grow as rapidly as the activity for which he is responsible. Eventually a point is reached where, although the man was exercising effective leadership when the activity was smaller, the organization begins to sense

73

the pressure not of his leadership but of his sitting placidly on top—in other words, his weight. He begins to make decisions when he is not adequately prepared. He stops listening to advice. He will say, "That's my decision and I want you to follow it." Once I heard one tell a subordinate, "I don't judge your loyalty to me by how well you carry out my good decisions but how well you carry out my bad decisions." I suggested to him that he rephrase that to say, "I judge your loyalty to me by how many bad decisions you permit me to make."

When the activity outgrows the man, you must recognize it and consider what action to take. Beware of moving too quickly. Be sure that you have thoroughly and completely evaluated the man, that he is not going through a temporary phase which often is caused by outside personal problems. Discuss it with him. Help him in every way you can. But if the problem persists, he must be replaced.

We have had a few cases in which we did not remove the man soon enough. It was costly to the company—not only in profit dollars but also in the lack of forward progress.

If the source of trouble is a man's built-in ceiling of capability, that man is the last to recognize or accept the fact. He can recognize almost any other problem, personal or otherwise, but when he is beginning to reach the limits of his ability he is reluctant to admit or accept it.

In this situation, one of two things must happen; either he must be transferred to a lesser job commensurate with his capabilities or he must be separated from the company. We have had to resort to the latter course on only a few occasions. Invariably the man himself leaves, often because of his pride.

On several occasions we have tried to reassign people who have not performed well to jobs of lesser responsibility that are within their demonstrated capabilities. Unfortunately, we have yet to find a satisfactory means of satisfying the individual in this manner. Sometimes the method will work for a while, but not indefinitely. This is a problem I hope can be solved some day. But I know of no solution on the horizon, although we have searched for it.

Another question I am often asked is: Who makes the best manager—an engineer, a salesman, a production man, a financial man, a lawyer, or what? You find some companies dominated by production people, which usually means the company president and others among his executives have come from a production background. The attitude in a production-oriented company is that if production personnel did not produce the product, the services of the design engineer, the marketing man, and the financial man would all be superfluous. Of course, the engineer, the salesman, the financial man, and other professional specialists can all say essentially the same thing about their own particular roles. And, more important, the inference is wrong. Domination by *any* one group is unhealthy in a progressive company and seldom works well over long periods.

Naturally, many people with engineering, scientific, legal, marketing, and production backgrounds have become outstanding management executives. But they did not fill all the key spots under them with engineers or salesmen or people from some other profession. Instead they maintained a balanced staff and a balanced organization in which individuals respected each others' skills and capabilities and could work together compatibly and effectively.

Some years ago a well-known company was organized by several top-notch scientists. All executive positions were held by scientists: the chairman of the board, the president, the executive vice president, and so forth. These men believed that a scientific organization should be run by scientists and therefore needed no one else around except secondary executives and clerks. The company did well for a few years as a small operation, but then it ran into trouble and had to be reorganized along different lines. While retaining a scientist as president, it became a balanced organization with more diversified talents in key positions. Significantly, it has since achieved success.

What about planning in a technologically based company? Is our scientific knowledge moving ahead so fast, people may ask, that a promising product may be technically leapfrogged and thus rendered obsolete before it can be produced and marketed? The pace of change is indeed a problem, of course, but it does not lessen the need for planning. To fail to plan is to stop progressing entirely or to travel in so many different directions that you neutralize all the motivating forces. But you must also have the kind of organization which is responsive to any changes in plans. *That* is the critical element, not the mechanics of planning.

It is also wise to have your research organization doing everything possible to make your own products obsolete. The reason is that internally exposed obsolescence will give you an early warning that a product's technology is being superseded on the outside. Without such warning, you may awaken some morning to find that a competitor already has the product on the market—and that can *really* be painful.

The Case for Bigness

In discussions of business organization these days, the question of conglomerates is almost always raised. What about mergers and acquisitions? What about bigness? Is all this good or bad for technologically based companies? Is it lessening competition in the United States? Does it restrict the growth of industry as a whole when a larger company absorbs a smaller company which might otherwise—at least theoretically—move ahead and achieve bigness on its own?

Let us look at the automobile industry as an example of past principles which still apply—at least in part—today. Over a period of time there have been upwards of 2,000 automobile companies in existence. If all of them—or even 500 or 200—had survived, compared with the half-dozen or so that we now have, it is very probable that we would still see more horses, buggies, and carriages in our streets than automobiles. The reason is simply that growth through mergers, acquisitions, and internal development has been necessary to provide the resources and capabilities for technological development of the automobile. It has also been necessary for meeting the requirements of the automobile market.

To be sure, Ford Motor Company did not grow by the merger route. While it bought Lincoln and one or two other companies, it forged ahead in its earlier days mostly by internal growth. But if it had not been for the mergers and acquisitions which made *other* automobile companies strong, Ford would have developed a monopoly years ago, over-running its small competitors. Had that happened, we might now have a modern version of the Model T, and all cars would be colored black.

Mergers and acquisitions thus have helped to create the strong automobile industry that we have today. Whether there should be four, six, or eight companies in competition with each other in an industry is beside the point. The important thing is that we need large companies, each in competition with the other.

In creating the immense automobile market, the automotive industry also created requirements for steel, rubber, oil, chemicals, fabric, machine tools, and materials of all kinds. As it stimulated and offered new horizons for those industries, the companies in them found they had to merge in order to meet the requirements of progress. They needed resources to improve their products, build more capacity, and create more jobs. In addition, new highways were built and whole new businesses came into existence.

Some incurable skeptics will interject at this point that perhaps we could do without all this burgeoning of industry. Let me answer them simply with questions: If the growth just described had not taken place, at what level would our gross national product be today? Would we have our present industrial base? Would we have had the industrial base needed for World War I and later for World War II? If not, would there be a free world today?

I am not sure that we have enough small companies in America; perhaps we need more. I am not sure that we have enough medium-sized companies; maybe we need more. But I am positive that we do not have enough large companies to provide real competition for the existing large companies, and to speed up and bring forward the new technologies that are influencing our lives as well as the hopes and strengths of this nation.

Limits on Growth?

Granted that growth and size are good things for business, may there still not be *too much* of these good things? For instance, I have been told that if Litton continues to maintain the 36% growth rate it maintained during much of the 1960's, it will rival the gross national product sometime around 1991. Is it not unlikely that Uncle Sam would allow this? If so, what about the long-term future of Litton Industries?

In terms of percentages, of course, there is a limit. But even though we have to report in those terms sometimes, we *think* in terms of absolute figures, and in that context we do see a continuing increase in our growth. There are not only exploding markets and technologies in our present lines of business, but potentials for such in fields that have been slower moving.

A good example of the latter is the shipbuilding industry. (Incidentally, this industry had, until recently, fewer mergers than almost any other industry in the United States.) Shipbuilding is largely subsidized by the government. In fact, the construction and operation of a merchant ship, even though a commercial product, is subsidized up to 50% of costs. Even so, in 1968 this country ranked fifteenth in the world in shipbuilding, four nations below Yugoslavia. While at the end of World War II we had 5,000 ships in our merchant marine, today we have less than 900, and 80% of them are either obsolete or no longer economical. There is even a question as to whether many will remain insurable in the near future.

In looking at various old-line companies in this industry, we at Litton concluded that many of them would become even weaker if they were not revitalized by technological and managerial innovations and new resources. We became interested in moving into this business. We set up a group of more than 200 scientists, engineers, and technicians—specialized in every field related to shipbuilding or shipping—to originate really new and advanced concepts for designing and producing ships. We are now building a new $130-million shipyard. It will be the most modern in the world. There is no question in our minds that an entirely new era in shipbuilding is imminent.

Different Versions of Progress

Business and industry today employ more than 70 million people in the United States, create about a million and a half new jobs every year, and are responsible for 84% of our gross national product. But ours is not a perfect system, and many people have not been satisfied with it. Some critics condemn industry, as well as technological change and technological progress, as a cause of many of our modern social ills. Others would do away with our private sector as it now exists—and have the government take over and guarantee all people a job, whether they want it or not.

I am reminded of a theory advanced a few years ago by a nonprofit institution. It predicted that by 1975 automation would limit the number of jobs in the United States to about 50 million and that more than 80 million people would need employment. It therefore proposed that everyone—worker and nonworker—be paid the same amount. The idea was received with much enthusiasm by many who wanted to get on the pay-no-work list. No one applied for the work category.

When a nation has achieved the tremendous progress which we are fortunate to have achieved in the United States, naturally there will be dislocations and imperfections. This does not mean that progress is bad; you cannot stop progress and say, "Let's take care of each little thing that has shown up as a dislocation." I say, let's keep moving and at the same time increase our efforts to resolve the problems which are a consequence of progress.

Business and industry can play an important role in these efforts. For example, a few years ago Litton began operating a Job Corps center. We had had experience in training many of our own employees, and had developed certain training techniques. So Litton and several other companies were asked by Sargent Shriver to bring our training skills to bear on a job-training program for young boys.

Most of the boys we trained came in with chips on their shoulders and with homemade knives and guns. Many wanted to fight, and as a result some buildings were set on fire. Many had previous criminal records, all were school dropouts, and a large percentage could not read or write. They represented all colors—white, black, red, and yellow.

We were concerned that some of the instructors we had carefully chosen to train the group might leave. Instead they rolled up their sleeves and went to work. The program was successful. By October 1968, for example, over 5,000 graduates from our Job Corps camp had found employment.

We seem to hear a great deal about boys who have not worked out, forgetting that many disadvantaged youth are now finding their way into the mainstream of America. Let me give you one example. Near the time these words were written, I was in Washington and arranged to take a graduate of our Job Corps camp to the White House to visit with the President. This boy came from a family of seven. He did not have a father at home, and his mother had been on relief for many years. He was a school dropout. When he went to our Job Corps center he would go behind the buildings and fight. He was big, weighed about 220, and was 19 years of age. With counseling service and other assistance, this young man began to change his interest and was motivated to prepare for his future.

His name was George Foreman and he was a Negro. Many Americans will remember seeing him on television or reading in the newspaper that he won the heavyweight boxing gold medal at the Olympics in 1968. He knocked out his Russian opponent in the second round and, following his victory, waved the American flag in the ring. When he was 16 he had little to look forward to; at 19 he had a General Educational Development diploma (the equivalent of a high school diploma), and possessed an employable trade as well as his boxing skill. He looked to the future with confidence and pride.

When people ask me if business has a responsibility to help those who have not shared in the country's economic growth, my answer is that of course it does. I think that business has the same interest in these people, and the same obligation to them, that government or anybody else has. It is true that when we talk about business, we talk about something generally considered to be impersonal and inanimate— called "it." But business is run by people, and all of management is people; 80% of the executives of U.S. corporations of all sizes come from small towns or modest backgrounds. They are just as human as anyone else; they are interested in the same things and concerned about the same things.

Need for Constructive Change

Earlier I mentioned the pace of change and progress in our nation. For purposes of illustration, let me try to compress the entire history of man into a period of 50 years. When we do this, it is startling to realize that man would not have had a permanent home the first 49 years of his life, and would have spent all of that time in a nomadic search for food. Only six months ago he would have learned to read and write. Two weeks ago he would have invented movable type, the microscope, and discovered circulation of the blood, the law of falling bodies, and the law of gravitation. Less than a week ago man would have discovered the application of electrical energy and the use of ether as an anesthetic, and invented the internal combustion engine, the gyroscope, the modern gun, sewing machine, telegraph, telephone, and typewriter. Twenty-four hours ago he would have been introduced to radio, TV, the airplane, automobile, motion picture, insulin, and vitamins. After lunch today he would have learned about radar, jet propulsion, the transistor, aureomycin, penicillin, and polio vaccine. A few minutes ago he would have boarded the first commercial jet airplane, and a few seconds ago he would have landed on the moon.

I have never heard any one express a desire to return to the nomadic life of those first 49 years. Nevertheless, many voices still decry the technical and economic progress that man has accomplished.

I certainly am not suggesting that we be satisfied with the present. If that were the case, progress would stop and the requirements of the future would never be met. At the same time, our dissatisfactions with the present must not tempt us to endorse ill-conceived or frivolous change just for the sake of change. This kind of change may create a smoke screen of activity but seldom, if ever, progress.

We must remember that progress has always caused some

dislocations, and we should be wary of the negative trap of condemning the whole, regardless of its value, because parts of it lack perfection. To destroy is to move backward. To build is to move forward. And we must move forward at an even faster pace than we are experiencing today.

To facilitate this progress, changes must be envisioned and accomplished, changes which are positive and realistic, changes which will not enlarge the very problems which we are attempting to minimize and solve. This is the role of modern business.

The task ahead is great, not only in America but in the world as well. During the careers of today's business students, the population of the world will more than double—from about 3¼ billion to more than 7 billion. Two-thirds of this increase will occur in areas where one-half of the people already have a standard of living at or below that necessary for human survival.

This is the people problem. It will be of such magnitude in its demands for food, housing, education, employment, and all the products of civilization, that it will require an expansion of business and industry, accompanied by vision and competent leadership, far beyond anything we can imagine today.

5

Technology and Business Opportunity for the International Business

By E. G. WOODROOFE
Chairman, Unilever, Ltd.

E. G. Woodroofe

E. G. Woodroofe is Chairman of Unilever, Ltd., Vice Chairman of Unilever N. V., and one of three members of the board of the company's Executive Committee. He was introduced to his Harvard Business School audience by Raymond Vernon, Herbert F. Johnson Professor of International Business Management. "The multinational enterprise with which Dr. Woodroofe is associated is regarded by most of us in the trade as the case of multinationalism par excellence," said Professor Vernon. "His career in itself makes interesting reading; it is so unlike the career contemplated by the average graduate of the Harvard Business School. Dr. Woodroofe has spent 30 years with his company, including a period as Director of Research, and he has operated on the technical end of the business for quite a long time. Because of his rather extraordinary blending of exposure to science and to a truly unusual company, he is in a position to tell us about the interplay between science, technology, and the multinational structure." From 1966 to 1968 Mr. Woodroofe was Chairman of the Research Committee of the Confederation of British Industry. In addition, he is a member of the Governing Body of the London Graduate School of Business Studies, and a member of the Court of Governors of the Administrative Staff College, Hendon.

Few economic developments promise to have as much impact on the future of the world economy as does the rise of the international business. American corporations have been most energetic in developing it, but it may command the most attention today in Europe. Let us begin this discussion, therefore, with some observations on the cause of the technological gap between Europe and the United States, and on Europe's effort to meet U.S. competition by building bigger companies with greater capabilities to exploit technological advances. Then let us examine the nature of a mature multinational company, whose management is open to the people of all countries in which it operates. No corporation has truly attained this form of organization yet, but Unilever and others are working in that direction. What are the steps to becoming a real multinational company? What are the advantages—and problems— of mixing people of different nationalities in a management group? How can a multinational company make itself welcome to a host country which needs it, yet may fear its power and motives? I shall discuss these and other questions.

Why Europe Got Behind

There have been epoch-making technical discoveries throughout the centuries, but right up to the Industrial Revolution they were largely fortuitous and infrequent. A sudden change came late in the eighteenth century when Great Britain was first to grasp the opportunities of technology and to blaze the trail of a new era. Great Britain led the world for many years, but her very success concealed from her the need to recognize that there was implicit in the Industrial Revolution a managerial revolution: that the change from a rural to an industrial economy called for new techniques in the management of men and resources. So it was left to the United States to initiate these techniques in the middle of the nineteenth century. U.S. industrialists were stimulated by an acute shortage of labor on the east coast as people were drawn west by the excitement of new frontiers.

The United States began leading the world in the development of business management skills, and still does. For a long time now in America, management has been considered a science to be studied, as well as an art to be acquired. Europeans awakened from their slumbers rather late in the day. As a consequence, the United States has a much greater proportion of well-managed companies than has Europe. Good management itself has stimulated technological progress in the United States. The commercial opportunities offered by advances in technology can be seized effectively only by those with high management skills. Indeed, advances in technology create the need for ever more sophisticated management skills.

Today, the technological gap between the United States and Europe has become a parrot cry. This gap is growing wider and causing considerable concern in Europe, so much so that there is a danger of technology becoming a cult divorced from the real task of producing economic growth. Yet the vitally important gap is not in technology but in management.

Although Europe lags in some fields of technology because it cannot afford to spend at the same levels as the United States does, nevertheless it has much to be proud of in its technological competence. For example, the United Kingdom can boast of achievements such as turbo and jet aero engines, radar, nuclear power, polythene, terylene, glass technology, and the synthesis of ammonia. But my purpose in mentioning these developments is not to comfort European pride. It is rather to point out that there are far too many instances in which Europe's inventive genius has produced ideas which have been followed up not in Europe *but in the United States.*

Why has this happened? Because technology alone is not

90

enough. The gap between the progress of the economies in the United States and Europe is due not so much to a lag in technological expertise as to differences in approach to education, particularly management education, coupled with a more aggressive attitude to business activities. The London *Times* has referred to this conclusion as "the gospel according to John Diebold."

Europe Courts Big Business

Management skills and a sizeable home market have enabled U.S. companies to lead the world in exploiting technology successfully. Many of these companies have grown, not only at home, but also internationally; and there is some concern that European economies might become dominated by these companies. Servan-Schreiber's recent book, *The American Challenge,* has sharpened this concern. The possibility of domination is stimulating Europe to think of meeting the American challenge by fostering the growth of its own big international companies.

For example, the French National Plan encourages mergers and envisages the formation of one or two companies of international size in each major section of industry. Again, in a recent speech, the Minister of Technology in the United Kingdom stated:

"The choice for us, it seems to me, lies between allowing these American corporations to pick up our growth points and integrate them as lesser parts of their own empires, or to start building viable units first on a national, then on an international basis, so that the companies that emerge are truly international in character and are not solely extensions of American industrial power with all the political implications that that would have."

To succeed, Europe-based international companies will, in

91

general, need to have the whole of Europe for their home market to match the immense home market of their American competitors. This need has inspired talk of introducing measures which will make it possible to form truly European companies answerable to one set of company and taxation laws. Unfortunately, it will be a long time before such proposals come to fruition. But other efforts might have earlier success. For instance, The Industrial Reorganisation Corporation sponsored by the British Government is interested in promoting mergers, including those across national boundaries. And there have been proposals for setting up a European Centre for Technology to stimulate the pooling of Europe's technological capabilities; this could lead to mergers, joint ventures, and working arrangements.

But competition is still the keenest spur of all, and in recent years the bogey man of U.S. competition has played a major part in stimulating mergers in Europe on an unprecedented scale. It is significant that these mergers have been mainly between firms in the same sectors of industry—and within nations, not across national boundaries. Even with this trend, however, only 61 European companies appear on the list of the 200 biggest industrial companies in *Fortune,* compared with 123 U.S. corporations.

Why have almost all European mergers taken place within national boundaries (with only a few exceptions, such as the merger of the photographic companies, Agfa, a German company, and Gevaert, a Belgian firm)? The main reason is the complications of corporation law and taxation law. They can make matters very difficult. To illustrate, Unilever has to operate on the basis of two companies in different countries—but the companies actually work as one. Between the two companies there is a series of agreements which equalize the rights of the shareholders. We need this arrangement in order to overcome the problems of a merger across a national boundary. In short, while it is possible to have mergers, management has to make special arrangements for them; otherwise the company is likely to encounter problems, especially of double taxation. Such difficulties notwithstanding, mergers across national boundaries will surely become more numerous in the future.

The American challenge is tending to force Europe to think of bigger companies, of international companies. For in the long term, if Europe fails in technological competition, each of its countries faces, as they see it, the choice of affluence with American economic domination, or a self-imposed lower standard of living with self-respect.

Let me emphasize I am not suggesting that the future lies only with the large company or that Europe's troubles are due entirely to its not having enough large companies. My point is that Europe needs an *adequate* quota of big international companies.

Incidentally, the technological ferment in Western Europe has aroused interest in the Soviet Union. The Russians have become eager to get together with other countries in Europe to exchange technical knowledge and licenses to use processes and to manufacture products. They have reached an agreement with the French. They have also been hosts to a trade delegation from the United Kingdom; I was a member of that delegation. The man heading the Russian side was a Deputy Prime Minister, and the other members were either ministers or deputy ministers. We agreed on areas (e.g., electrical engineering) in which we had a common interest. Working parties were set up between the Russians and us to see whether they had anything which they could license to Britain, whether Britain had anything she could license to the Soviet Union, and whether it was possible to set up joint research projects.

I think there is no doubt that the Russians are conscious of the fact that they are good scientists, and they are doing some very good scientific work. But they have not developed the capability of applying their know-how to the needs of the community. They see that in the West this capability has been developed, so their idea is to try and put together their scientific genius with the genius of the West for applying science to the needs of the community.

Conditions of Success

If Europe is to succeed in its resolve to promote the growth of international companies by exploiting technology successfully, it must apply the same golden rules for success to its companies as Americans do to their companies. It must use the necessary management skills to improve products, develop new ones, improve methods of production, modify organization patterns, and set up effective means of communication. And to improve the general capability of management, it needs to have more management training. It needs to have more engineers and perhaps fewer scientists. It needs to have a greater proportion of people educated to a higher level so that an executive can delegate down the line more than is done now (more as is done in the United States). In the United States, as I remember, of all those people eligible to go to a university, more than 40% actually do go. Perhaps many of them fall out in the first year, but, nevertheless, 40% compares with a figure of less than 10% for the United Kingdom.

But the international company needs to do more. Not only does it have the world's market as its oyster, with all the advantages of size, but it also has far greater opportunities to benefit from the advances of world technology. How are those opportunities to be grasped?

First and foremost, the enterprise must be not just an international company but *a mature multinational company*—a stage which, so far as I know, no company has yet reached. The organization must not merely be large and do business in many countries. It must also be run by the nationals of many countries. It must have progressed beyond the stage where it sends

94

its export salesmen out from home, or runs its overseas subsidiaries by expatriates. It must have progressed even beyond the stage where there are local nationals in the top management echelons of these subsidiaries. It must have progressed to the stage where its management posts throughout the world are *equally open to the citizens of all the countries in which it operates.*

The Road to Multinationality

My company, Unilever, started along the road to multinationality at the turn of the century. Lord Leverhulme, the founder of the British half of what was to become an Anglo-Dutch company, set the note when he declared at the opening of the Olten factory of his subsidiary company in Switzerland: "I unhesitatingly say that it is not within the range of man's ability to train a staff of employees in one country capable of attending to all the details of a business carried on in another country."

Since that time, the company has made considerable progress towards becoming truly multinational, and progress continues. We manufacture and sell in nearly 60 countries. In 1950, in our companies outside Europe and North America, 50% of the management was expatriate—which we thought far too high. Now it is down to 13%. The obverse of the coin is that in Western Europe, 8% of our managers are working in Unilever's European subsidiaries outside their own countries. Our joint Head Offices in London and Rotterdam have managers from 10 European countries and a few men, some in senior posts, from such other parts of the world as Australasia, Canada, Africa, and India—and this in spite of the British and Dutch taxation systems which are no encouragement to managers of other nationalities to make the move.

While the benefits of a policy of multinationality are felt

throughout the whole range of a company's activities, nowhere is the potential reward so rich and worthwhile as in harnessing technology. The talents, the flair, the intuitive thinking, and the points of view of many different cultures can be brought to bear on a problem, whether it is one of science, management, organization, or consumer response. But, of course, it is not easy to do this, for if people from many cultures are to work effectively together, they must also acquire for themselves some common language of communication, some common culture.

For instance, it is not enough for Unilever to appoint Indians to manage our Indian business, as we have done with considerable success, or to bring Germans into head office jobs in London or Rotterdam. We must do this within the context of an overall Unilever way of doing things—what in America would be called a business philosophy. I must emphasize that the Unilever way is not an Anglo-Dutch philosophy, but one to which *all* nationalities have contributed: one which Englishmen and Dutchmen have to absorb just as much as do Brazilians or Swedes. I mean that in giving advice, in setting out company policy, or in reporting on marketing campaigns, technical developments, or political changes, there is (or should be) an accepted way of doing things which is readily understood in *all* parts of the Unilever world. Moreover, this pattern of behavior is not simply imposed from the center. Rather, its elements have been drawn from all parts of the organization, and they have been crystallized by the center.

I emphasize this because it is a point that has been driven home to us as a result of having two head office nationalities. In 1929, the Dutch Margarine Union and the British Lever Brothers merged to form Unilever. In the beginning, as a matter of policy, most rooms in the head office had in them one Dutchman and one Englishman. Mutual respect and understanding were fostered by this planned mingling of the two groups. For one thing, it is much more difficult to dislike some-

96

body you see than somebody you don't see. For another, characteristic modes of expression are assimilated better. We learned a very long time ago that when an Englishman says, "I am afraid I do not entirely agree," he means exactly the same as a Dutchman does when he says, "I absolutely disagree." Expand this to the way each nationality expresses shades of meaning and to many nationalities, and you get some idea of what I mean by mutual understanding.

I often wonder whether large U.S. corporations do enough to develop this kind of understanding. When they "Americanize" employees, do some U.S. organizations tend to lose something of the variety of ideas which might otherwise be brought to them by nationals of other countries?

Our business philosophy at Unilever—let's call it "Unileverisation"—does not represent an attempt to create some new citizenship. However good an Italian or a Dane may be as a Unilever manager, clearly he will still think and feel on many subjects like an Italian or a Dane. Indeed, he is likely to be of little use to us if he does not. One of the main advantages of a multinational staff is that one always has somebody who understands the local market by instinct as well as by market research. Expatriates may be able to find out by proper enquiry what the local customer needs and how he should be approached; and the more imaginative of them may on occasion be able to achieve a real empathy with the countries to which they are posted. But instinctive market understanding will come much easier to a man with local roots.

Opening More Gates to Knowledge

Knowledge is international. Sooner or later any major scientific discovery in one country becomes known in all countries. But it is often later than sooner, and if one wishes to avoid this time lag, there must be an intimate relationship with

97

the academic community which is doing the research. One must be able to talk to academics in their universities, to meet them in their homes, to read their books and articles in the languages in which they are first published. A researcher, whether studying physics or sociology, talks more easily to somebody he is familiar with as part of his own community than to somebody he perceives as an outsider, perhaps even as a greedy foreigner. This is particularly true if his work has commercial significance.

Clearly, no company is big enough to produce all the knowledge it can use. It has to be able to tap the knowledge of the wider community around it. Today that wider community covers the whole world. Science is no longer the preserve of a few nations. Rich countries make major contributions because they alone can afford to pay the costs of large-scale research and, in particular, development. But nearly every country contributes to scientific research—and this includes some of the developing nations. For instance, we in Unilever have a very effective research laboratory in India that does valuable work in both research and development.

A multinational company is likely to obtain a synergistic effect from its different research and development operations around the world. In our company we find that much scientific knowledge spills over from one product to another. Although we are in detergents, toiletries, fatty chemistry, foods, and so on—areas that may seem quite separate—we find that they are interconnected. Flavors are involved in many of these projects; surface chemistry comes into many of them; and numerous other examples could be given. We thus gain an enormous amount of synergism from the effects of the science in one field influencing another. Such effects are enhanced by being multinational.

An additional incentive to multinational growth is the fact that, without it, a company may find it increasingly difficult to tap the knowledge and know-how of countries in which it does not operate. In the past, U.S. companies, with characteristic vigor, exploited (in the best sense of the word) many of the world's discoveries and took a clear lead in innovation. For example, the first computer was built in Germany in 1940, Britain pioneered the technical development, but the United States dominates the world market; and penicillin was discovered in Britain but developed technically and commercially in the first instance by U.S. organizations.

It has taken Europe a long time to recognize the situation for what it is, yet to none have its implications come home more than to major European companies. Now that they are alerted, as are organizations in other parts of the world, all of them desire to see their own discoveries developed in their own countries. This is why it will not be as easy in the future as it was in the past to find discoveries of one country available for commercial development in another. Not only are local companies likely to be more aggressive in grasping these opportunities, and particularly so as the standard of management improves, but governments are also taking action. For example, the role of the National Research Development Corporation, set up in Britain in 1948, is to develop British inventions of seemingly good potential that come out of local universities, government laboratories, or from private inventors—inventions which otherwise might not be taken up. The government backs the corporation with money. There is nothing insular in this: only an urge to reap the benefit of local talents for the ultimate benefit of all.

One is tempted to think it possible to keep in touch with world developments in science and technology simply by getting the company's head office staff to monitor the research which is published around the world, and perhaps also by using staff experts and other people on tour from headquarters to talk to local scientists. In practice, this is not enough. A company needs a closer and more intimate touch. In particular, it needs local representation in the form of facilities and staffs.

People talk much more freely, new ideas and the significance of new developments are discussed with much more mutual understanding, if those doing the talking are citizens of the same country. After all, their backgrounds of education and culture, of usages and conventions, of patterns of thought and modes of expression, are the same. The members of an international company which is equipped to develop local ideas and inventions in its local development laboratories or factories are more readily welcomed by academics, government research workers, and other inventors. The inventor or the man with new ideas naturally prefers to see them developed in his own country. So an international company, properly organized, can serve both national aspirations and international prosperity.

In Unilever, we feel that we are able to draw strength from the presence of company research or development laboratories in 33 of the countries in which we operate. Some of these laboratories are very large and sophisticated units; some are quite small, their main purpose being to modify the products developed by the main research laboratories to suit local conditions. Both types enable us to keep in touch with the local scientific and technological community.

Understanding Markets

To be represented in many countries is even more useful in the interplay between social sciences and technology than in the purely physical sciences, in marketing than in production. Markets, at least in the developed parts of the world, are getting more alike all the time, yet history, tradition, taste, the distribution of income, the taxation system, and a hundred other causes still mean that the pattern of consumer needs in one country can be very different from that of another. Sometimes one simply has to adapt oneself to this difference; sometimes one may get an idea from a consumer need which stands

100

out clearly in one country, and apply it to other countries where that need is still latent. For instance, washing products which include enzymes to break down the proteinaceous dirt on clothes were recently developed in the Netherlands, where the habit of pre-soaking clothes before washing was widespread and the advantages of enzymes were therefore obvious. Today enzyme products are successful also in the United States, where there is hardly any pre-soaking and where, therefore, the consumer need for enzyme products was by no means obvious.

Some countries offer particular advantages for certain types of market testing. As an illustration, if one wishes to launch a product which involves the consumer in real novelty, the United States is a very favorable market in which to do it. Similarly, if one wishes to sell something which saves the housewife's time, though at a cost which puts a fairly high value on the time saved, there is no housewife more willing to pay the price than the American housewife.

But there are other products for which the United States is a less suitable country in which to pioneer. The British, for instance, are much keener on gardening, much more interested in trying out anything which will give them more beautiful flowers and more luscious lawns. But that has to be on a do-it-yourself basis, and so there is a good market in England for labor-saving garden gadgetry. Again, when the Italians applied their flair for design to motor scooters in the late 1940s' they achieved instant success through the whole of Europe; but motor scooters are of little account in America.

Differences in tariffs or in the availability of raw materials can send product development off on different lines in different countries, creating unusual marketing advantages in the process. Germany, for instance, is ahead in the use of fabricated unplasticized polyvinylchloride, usually called PVC. Rigid PVC has the marked advantage of noncorrosion. Germany achieved its leadership in an effort to husband its resources of metal. The United States is the leading market for plasticized PVC, but it is only slowly becoming aware of the attractions of *un*plasticized PVC. Yet the latter is likely to take off some day in the American market, and when it does, a company which has learned to use it in Germany might find itself in a position of very considerable advantage. Moreover, Japan, which has expanded its production of PVC at a fantastic rate over the last 10 years, has developed modified PVC products with very attractive specialized properties to suit her own requirements.

Again, we in Unilever have learned in India, because of the foreign exchange shortage there, how to process vegetable oils which had not previously been used commercially, and how to tailor others to new uses. The technology which has been developed might well help us in other countries in years to come. To cite another illustration still, because Australia has a plentiful supply of tallow while other oils and fats have to be imported, the stimulation to develop new techniques for processing tallow is greater there than in most other countries.

Some Broad Characterizations

Each nationality has its recognizable characteristics—its spectrum of virtues and vices—superimposed on the infinite variation amongst human beings. We are conditioned by our experience, conventions, and accepted beliefs and standards drilled into us at mother's knee, in school, in universities, in business. The scientist, the technologist, and the manager are all subject to the influences, each in his own way. Let me make some broad characterizations of a few nationalities.

The Britisher excels in intuitive leaps forward; he is quick to grasp a hypothesis; he tolerates and enjoys that "state of muddled suspense that precedes a great inductive generalization." It is probably this trait which gives the British scientist his place at the head of the league table of major nations for Nobel prizes per unit of population. But he flinches from writing down

102

terms of reference and from organizing himself. To him this is to restrict freedom of thought. He must have loopholes of escape from his own conclusions. Even the British constitution is not a written document.

The *Dutchman*, in contrast to the Britisher, likes to map out a framework, to set down terms of reference. His progress is much more logical than that of his British colleague, and he is less likely to leave "stones unturned." It is second nature to him to make the best use of such resources as are available, not surprisingly perhaps, since even some of the land on which he lives had to be wrested from the sea. Little wonder, he says, that "God made the earth but the Dutch made Holland." Perhaps it was the infinite capacity for taking pains and the canny approach to financial matters, which the Dutch share with the Scots, that accounted for their great success in exporting their banking skills into the City of London in the late seventeenth century (when, for example, they played a major part in providing not only the capital for the foundation of the Bank of England, but also a considerable element of the technical knowledge required to run it).

The *Frenchman* is intuitive, like the Britisher. His love of logic is proverbial, even more so than the Dutchman's. He is certainly more temperamental and more conservative than either. He is the leavener of the international scene—at least, when he is not being too insular.

The *American* has an almost aggressive vigor with which he seizes on and expands new ideas, boldly takes risks, and goes for quick results. This vigor is unmatched anywhere in the world and, together with the American's strong sense of purpose, pace, and urgency, is one of the major reasons for the economic strength of the United States.

More Sparkle with Mixed Nationals

Now, to have such national talents brought to bear on a company's problems, and to have different nationals seeking to spark off new ideas, greatly enhances the chances of corporate success. This is one of the reasons that Unilever prefers to have major research laboratories in a number of countries, with company development units scattered throughout the whole world, rather than one big central R & D laboratory. Yet that kind of step alone falls short of the need.

If employing different national groups on problems gives sparkle to a company, employing groups of *mixed* nationalities enhances the sparkle. As already indicated, many management groups in Unilever are of mixed nationalities; this mixing is a matter of conscious policy. Numerous project groups and working parties are organized in this manner. Research workers are sent to work for long spells in company laboratories outside their own country. The planning of a man's career often includes an appointment to a job outside his own country as a deliberate part of the development of his managerial or technological skills. This gives him experience in working with other nationalities and helps remove some of the blinders put on him (as on all of us) by the characteristics of his nationality. When people work willingly and closely together, each can see the strengths and weaknesses of his own approach and that of his "foreign" colleague. The Dutchman can see that he organizes too much, and the Britisher can see the wisdom of organizing himself more.

Moreover, the interaction of intuitive and logical approaches often produces results which, in isolation, neither would produce. The foreigner comes in and asks all the questions the local takes for granted—a boon because there is no greater barrier to innovation than cliché thinking, and we are all guilty of it.

Generally speaking, the foreigners who make up part of a

104

work group are in that country for a limited time only—perhaps five to eight years. Few are likely to be permanent members. The company counts on the nationals to provide intuitive understanding of local markets, institutions, and customs.

I must stress that the interactions and synergy described come about only if morale is high. If it is low, national differences between members are likely to appear as obstructions of outlook and to breed mutual suspicion and hostility; whereas if it is high, such differences appear more as interesting contrasts of vocabulary and sources of strength in problem solving (especially when the managers concerned have a high level of professional skill).

There is another and even more compelling reason for employing men in management positions outside their own countries: this practice enables a company to choose the best man for a vacancy from a vastly greater pool of talent than would otherwise exist. The general standard of management is thereby raised and morale gets a boost. In Unilever, Ceylon is proud to have provided a manager for Ghana, and Ghana in turn is proud to have provided a manager for the Solomon Islands. Moreover, more bright and ambitious young men (particularly those from the smaller countries) are attracted to join the company because of the enhanced promotion prospects.

Creating Mutual Advantages

There are immense advantages in being a multinational company, as I have indicated; but there are difficulties, too. In many parts of the world, there is growing concern about the influence of big international companies, and there has been talk of neo-colonialism. This trend has been over-dramatized by some academics, but nevertheless it is real. To be big and to be loved seems to be against nature. One objection is that large multinational companies are accountable to no political

105

authority. In addition, their ultimate loyalty has been questioned, as has their power to frustrate the aspirations of the countries in which they operate. Small nations feel helplessly dependent on the companies' research and development activities, while bigger nations fear that the enterprises batten on national technology without contributing towards it. The more advanced and exclusive is the technology of a company, the more is it welcomed by a host country—the greater also is its bargaining power and the greater the apprehension of the host.

An international company must be sensitive to these feelings and must have concern for the welfare of the host country. The relationship should be one of mutual give-and-take. However, it is not sufficient for a company to give only by bringing into a country its capital, its technology, and its management skills. This it does to the great benefit of the economic progress of the country, but it must also contribute to technological and managerial progress *in that country*. The international company is an instrument for spreading technology around the world only if it employs some local technologists who thereby participate in the general advance of technology and, better still, does some of its research or development work outside the base country. Its scientists and technologists should truly belong to three communities—the scientific ranks of their own country, the organization of the international company, and the scientific world community.

By employing nationals in the topmost management positions in its subsidiary companies—nationals who are responsible to international headquarters for commercial matters but are loyal and accountable to their own governments—the international company can show a genuine desire to be a good citizen wherever it operates. Of course, "foreigners" to an area will be employed there, too, but this should offer no problem so long as the "foreigners" are not solely nationals from the home base of the international company, and so long as there are no "second-class citizens." An economy can be strengthened if its businesses are managed in part by foreign managers, with their different approaches to problems, and in part by nationals who have had their outlook broadened by working abroad.

Adopted widely, the multinational approach could create a significant unifying force in a world torn by the disruptive forces of rising nationalism, international suspicion, and misunderstanding. Moreover, this force will become stronger as more countries spawn more international companies. The concern felt around the world about the activities of international companies breeds protective and restrictive policies. If the behavior of these companies helps to allay some of this concern, this will do much to promote a liberal attitude to international investment and a square deal for the investor. The answer to getting the world's technology effectively harnessed to meet the world's needs is surely to encourage the investments of the technologically advanced companies on a global scale. But the trend must be for these companies to become more international, more multinational, and less subject to purely nationalistic influences. The more widely their ownership can be spread, so that people in many places can participate in their success, the less likely is it that their activities will be curbed by nationalistic restrictions.

6

NASA as an Adaptive Organization

By JAMES E. WEBB
Administrator of NASA, 1961–1968

James E. Webb

James E. Webb is best known to Americans as Administrator of the National Aeronautics and Space Administration (NASA) during a period of unprecedented accomplishment—from February 1961 to October 1968. Prior to his assuming the top post at NASA he had served the U.S. Government as Director of the Bureau of the Budget from 1946 to 1949, Undersecretary of State from 1949 to 1952, and in various other positions. From 1953 to 1958 he was President of Republic Supply Company in Oklahoma, and Chairman of the Board of that company from 1958 to 1960.

He was introduced to his audience at the Harvard Business School in September, 1968 by Donald K. Price, Dean of the John F. Kennedy School of Government at Harvard. "I have had the privilege of working for James Webb and with him for a good many years," Dean Price said. "His competence to speak to you on the relationship of technology and management comes not merely from his position as leader for the past several years of the most challenging and intricate job of civilian management that I can think of in history. It comes also from his awareness of the way in which that job of technological management is a part of the intricate network of relationships between government and business and between government and educational institutions. It is a system that needs to be appreciated not only in terms of technological and economic efficiency—although it requires that—but also in terms of business and scientific statesmanship."

$\mathbf{I}$N a commencement address at Colorado College in June, 1957, I thought to stimulate the graduates by repeating a speculative timetable for space exploration that Mr. J. S. McDonnell of St. Louis had laid out two weeks before at the Missouri School of Mines. I quoted Mr. McDonnell in these terms:

"In about a dozen years or so, we will launch a satellite that will circle the earth and moon.

"By about 1980, we will have made sufficient advances to permit the launching of a satellite that will circle the earth and Mars.

"By about 1990, we can go forward to the point of launching a space ship carrying human beings which will circle the earth for an extended period as a satellite and return safely."

Today we all know how much these predictions—well-informed ones, at the time—underestimated what both the USSR and the United States could do. Four months later Sputnik flew, and in four years Gagarin had circled the earth and returned—not in the year 1990 but in 1961. In May, 1961, President John F. Kennedy summoned this nation to an expanded and accelerated effort to achieve for the United States the status of a spacefaring nation second to none. The nation's goal of a moon landing by 1970 was met with months to spare.

What was accomplished by that effort? What was learned? Let us look briefly at (1) the technical and organizational capabilities the United States developed, then in detail at (2) the management know-how gained from our space program. The latter, while not having the glamor of the technical accomplishments, is also a very important and enduring asset. If leaders in business, government, science, engineering, and education take full advantage of it, many other goals can be brought closer to achievement. Important lessons can be learned from NASA's experience about the best way to start an ambitious new program which is under great public pressure to "produce"; about an effective legislative base for such a program; about the choice of objectives where there is much uncertainty and many differing viewpoints; about effective policies for working with other organizations in government, education, and business; about planning for changing conditions, technological as well as political; and about other important matters. I shall comment on these lessons in this chapter, bearing in mind their potential usefulness for large transportation, urban development, communication, oceanographic, welfare, and other types of public programs.

Capabilities Built Up

I do not need to review here the successes of the Mercury, Gemini, and Apollo programs; they have been well publicized in the newspapers and on TV. But it is important to get across an understanding of the *capabilities* built up during the 1960's. A good way to do this is to review NASA's launch activities during just one week of one year.

Let us take the second week in November 1967. Admittedly it was a full week. But what was done then can be repeated and on an even grander scale. The capabilities demonstrated that week are *lasting* capabilities. We may never use them to the fullest, or even in large part, but they do exist and can be put to use any time if not permitted to deteriorate below the minimum for reactivation.

Monday, November 6. On this day NASA launched an Applications Technology Satellite—the ATS III. This was put into an earth-synchronous orbit over the South Atlantic, which means that the satellite hovers 24 hours a day over the same spot. Since that Monday in November, 1967, the satellite has been sending back color pictures of the earth and its atmosphere and serving as an experimental communications relay station. This machine will stay in position for a long time. It

114

is continuously adding to our knowledge of the earth, its weather, the effects of the sun's energy on nature's processes here on earth, and how to increase efficiency in long-distance communications.

In understanding and predicting weather, the measurements made by the ATS and other NASA experimental spacecraft, added to the regular 24-hours-per-day operations now performed by ESSA's space systems, are even at this early time in space development providing a handsome return on the time and money invested. Some continually transmit cloud-cover pictures as they circle the earth, and any weather station in any nation or on any ship has only to use an inexpensive receiver to get this up-to-the-minute and on-location weather information. This service is one way our country says to every other country, every day, that we as a people want to use our new power over the forces of nature in a joint effort with them, with benefits to both of us, and not to threaten or to coerce them to follow some pattern laid down by us. It is our way of saying that we want to develop power together with them, not power over them.

Tuesday, November 7. Our second launch of the week, Surveyor VI, came on this day. Two days after launch, this second-generation lunar spacecraft made a soft landing on the moon and promptly began to transmit detailed pictures of a very rugged stretch of the lunar surface. This launch was one of a series of unmanned launches of automated systems that included Ranger and Lunar Orbiter as well as Surveyor. As many people will remember, the Rangers came directly in for a crash landing, taking large numbers of pictures of a limited area right up to the point of contact. As for the Lunar Orbiter series, all five of them were outstandingly successful. They circled the moon at about 27 miles, providing a complete map of the moon, both front and back, with excellent resolution. The Surveyors were the soft-landers. They rounded out the work of Lunar Orbiter and Ranger. Many people have seen them on

115

TV digging holes on the moon, making chemical analyses of the soil, and blasting small craters with their jet engines.

Surveyor VI, launched on Tuesday, was moved from one place to another eight feet away—the first, very short, but significant rocket flight on the surface of the moon. Just as the Ranger pictures provided details 1,000 times more precise than earth-based telescopes, Surveyor pictures provided astronomers with a further improvement in resolution, by another factor of 1,000 times. With this kind of capability, the way was opened for lunar and planetary investigations of a type and scope undreamed of before we learned to use rocket technology.

Thursday, November 9. This was the date of the first test-launch of the Saturn V. The first aim of this test was to make sure that this powerful booster could develop the full 7.5 million pounds of thrust needed when our Apollo astronauts started their round-trip journey to the moon, or when we decide to send a 10,000 pound payload to Mars. A second objective was to make sure that the heat shield on the Apollo spacecraft could withstand the temperature, deceleration, and pressures of re-entry into the earth's atmosphere at 25,000 miles per hour. A third aim was to make sure that the $500 million Saturn-Apollo launch complex at Cape Kennedy, and the global tracking and data acquisition network we had been building, could handle the job of automatically launching this gigantic machine and remotely controlling its complex mission.

Saturday, November 11. The last launch of the week—ESSA IV—came on this day, from the Western Test Range in California. ESSA IV was launched into an orbit that passes near both the North and South Poles and is so synchronized with the rotation of the earth that it can observe and report on the entire earth's weather in daylight every 24 hours. This is known as a polar-retrograde orbit, so that as the earth turns the satellite progresses backward just enough so that it always passes over a point on the earth in maximum sunlight to take its pictures and make its measurements. (The orbit is also called sun-synchronous.) The ESSA IV launch differed from the three earlier launches during the week in that it exemplified not the pioneering done by NASA at the frontier of technology and science, but the way in which space operations had become a routine contributor of essential services for the benefit of everyone. ESSA IV is a standard workhorse machine which the U.S. Weather Bureau uses in its day-to-day task of studying and forecasting the weather. It uses this satellite just as it uses weather reporting ships, planes, and balloons. However, the utility of ESSA IV is far beyond anything we can achieve in any other way. It works 24 hours a day, all around the world, and feeds information into something like 296 stations in the United States and about 86 stations in 45 other countries. It is truly a working bird.

Significance of Achievement

The space capabilities demonstrated in the second week of November 1967 represent—or can be parlayed into—better than 90% of everything we need to carry out almost any mission that even the most daring have placed on our space agenda for the next decade.

How important are these capabilities? There are many different views on this question. For my own part, I do not believe our nation could have long continued as a great power if we had not built up the means to conduct operations in space —if we had instead conceded a monopoly of this new dimension of man's activity to the U.S.S.R. or any other country. I believe we would have sacrificed our chances to keep pace in the technological competition that is the crucial test of our times. We would have turned our backs on the opportunities space offers for large extensions of scientific knowledge. We would have denied to ourselves tools and knowledge that have an important bearing on numerous problems that beset us and the rest of mankind.

Of those who are skeptical of this view, I would simply ask: Had NASA not developed these capabilities, how would the outside world look to us today? How would we look to the outside world? What would our people think of our leaders and of themselves? *What would our future be?*

The space story is significant in another way. There is, as suggested earlier, the matter of *how* as well as *what.* The *way* in which we have built up our space capabilities, and what we have learned in the process about the *requirements for success* in such long-scale endeavors, may constitute as important a contribution to our nation—to its ability to move forward into the future—as do the technical capabilities themselves.

In the NASA program, it has been demonstrated that a combination of 400,000 industry, university, and government workers can coordinate their efforts successfully in the most complex, large, technical undertaking the human race has yet attempted. This demonstration has unusual significance at a time when we are asking how the other great and fateful tasks that loom so large before us—urban renewal, health and welfare, better transportation, pollution control, and ocean development, to name but a few—will be carried out.

To succeed in the space program, we have had to learn and apply new ways of organizing and administering human and material resources. The hard fact of modern organizational life is that traditional patterns and procedures cannot meet today's needs for overcoming society's pressing problems or for keeping pace in a purposeful way with accelerating technological change.

118

Limits of Bureaucracy

The feature that has hitherto most strongly marked large-scale organized activity in our society has been the trend toward ever larger and more ponderous bureaucracies. This is evident in both the private and public sectors. Admittedly, for many lines of endeavor bureaucracies work reasonably well. Where the job is routine or repetitive, the mechanistic approach of the bureaucracy is probably suitable since it is both safer and surer.

But where the job is new and different, where it involves coping with uncertainty and rapid change, where it requires a first use of new knowledge and new technology, where it is concerned with new and shifting demands, where it is dependent for success on highly skilled and sensitive individuals with varied types of expertise—there the bureaucratic approach falls down, and hard. Its structure is almost by definition inflexible. It can, as the historian William H. McNeill has pointed out, "only do what it was built to do." [1] Its effectiveness is in almost direct ratio to the degree of stability that prevails within itself and in the surrounding environment. When pressures arise for change in its goals, its way of doing things, or its role, it can hardly respond lest it destroy itself. Built-in mechanisms neutralize the pressures, whether they come from within or from without. To quote McNeill again:

"Scientific personal classification allows, nay, requires, interchangeability of parts in the bureaucracy; hence individual appointments and dismissals make remarkably little difference. . . . The administrative totality, its overall structure and functioning, and even the general lines of policy remain almost unaffected by changes of elected officials. Even energetic reformers, placed in high offices and nominally put in charge of such vast bureaucratic hierarchies,

1. William H. McNeill, *The Rise of the West* (Chicago, University of Chicago Press, 1963), p. 803.

119

find it all but impossible to do more than slightly deflect the line of march.

"A really massive bureaucracy . . . becomes a vested interest greater and more strategically located than any 'private' vested interest in the past. Such groupings are characterized by a lively sense of corporate self-interest, expressed through elaborate rules and precedents, and procedures rising toward the semi-sacredness of holy ritual. These buttress a safe conservatism of routine and make modern bureaucracy potentially capable of throttling back even the riotous up-thrust of social and technical change nurtured by modern science." [2]

The type of job with which NASA was charged in the National Aeronautics and Space Act of 1958 is clearly beyond the capability of a traditional bureaucratic establishment. It requires above everything flexibility. It cannot be accomplished by an organization that is rigid either in structure or in methods. It can be done only by an organization that is truly adaptive, that can:

—Deal with the unknown.
—Operate under conditions of rapid change in a turbulent environment.
—Secure and act upon instantaneous feedback from both its own performance and its environment.
—Use and where necessary generate new knowledge and new technology.
—Combine and recombine highly trained experts of differing backgrounds and disciplines.
—Adjust to varying levels of support.
—Speed up and slow down.
—Change directions in mid-course.
—Constantly improvise, invent, and innovate.

Dr. Warren G. Bennis describes this need in terms of "adaptive, problem-solving, temporary systems of diverse specialists,

2. *Ibid.*

120

linked together by coordinating executives in organic flux."[3] Mr. Harvey Sherman describes it in much the same way: ". . . the problem we now face in organization may well have changed in nature from one of adjusting organizations to meet present conditions; that is, maintaining equilibrium, to one of adjusting organizations to meet future unknown conditions; that is maintaining desired dis-equilibrium." [4]

Is NASA Approach Applicable?

Some contend that the experiences NASA has gained in organizing and administering the nation's aeronautics and space programs have little applicability to other large, complex, and difficult tasks we face. For instance, *Forbes* has voiced such skepticism:

"Can these systems [that NASA has employed] be applied to problems other than those of space and of the military? A good deal has been said and written on the subject. Much of it is sheer propaganda, intended to justify space exploration and to try to gain a beachhead for aerospace companies in non-aerospace businesses. Only this January, for example, an article in *Fortune* expounded: 'The systematic planning that built missiles and spacecraft can be used with telling effect to attack urban complexities.' The argument ran that the systems approach can be applied to earthly problems: transportation bottlenecks, hardcore unemployment, the pollution of water and air.

"But *can* it? This is open to serious doubt. Space exploration deals chiefly with nature and technology—nonhuman forces. The more earthly problems basically involve interrelations among people: We already know, technologically speaking, what the problems are and how to solve them. We do not know how to get people to accept the solutions or how to allocate the costs. . . .

3. "New Patterns of Leadership for Tomorrow's Organizations," *Technology Review*, April 1, 1968, p. 37.

4. Harvey Sherman, *It All Depends: A Pragmatic Approach to Organization* (University, Ala., University of Alabama Press, 1966), p. 27.

". . . systems engineering is simply the planned, organized undertaking of unusually big, unusually complex engineering projects. A great deal can be learned from it. To oversell it, however, to promise some kind of alchemy from it—like so much of the other overselling involved in the space program—is a real disservice to the basic values of space exploration." [5]

These comments, it seems to me, rest upon an oversimplification of the process NASA has used in organizing and administering the space program. As for the "systems approach" and its various sub-elements, such as "systems analysis," "systems engineering," and "systems management," I agree and have repeatedly emphasized that much of what is said represents myth rather than reality. These are all useful tools. They greatly increase our ability to get things done. But they also have their limitations and pitfalls, and any idea that they can give us an assured way to lead and manage large and complex enterprises is fanciful in the extreme.

The NASA programs have made very effective use of the systems approach; they could not have succeeded without it. But our effort has involved much more than the systems approach, much more than the capability of any computer yet dreamed of. It is incorrect to say, as *Forbes* does, that space exploration deals chiefly with "nature and technology" and hence contrasts with "more earthly problems" that "basically involve interrelationships among people." Space exploration is indeed concerned with natural forces and with the technology needed to measure and use these forces. But it has required the coordinated work of 20,000 industrial enterprises, 200 universities, and 400,000 highly skilled men and women, including hundreds of leading scientists, engineers, and managers. It has involved welding together many pre-existing organizations, all established under differing circumstances and for different purposes, and all with their own separate practices and methods.

5. *Forbes*, July 1, 1968, p. 91.

It has involved learning to work within the framework of our representative governmental system of decision making and under the constant glare of the TV cameras. It has involved keeping the people of the nation and their elected representatives informed of what NASA is doing, how, and to what ends. It has involved safeguarding basic values in our society and respecting its preferred ways of doing things. It has involved keeping a close weather eye out for unexpected impacts. And it has involved meeting the unending need to ensure the financial support necessary to keep the whole enterprise going.

The secret of NASA's achievements is not a discovery of new knowledge and technology (most of the basic knowledge and technology needed were already at hand) but an approach to organizing and managing available knowledge and technology in a purposeful and effective way. This, fundamentally, has been a job of organizing and managing *people*—and communicating with the public and legislative representatives.

Much the same kind of job is needed in other areas. I share *Forbes'* doubts that we will have to discover new knowledge or to invent new technology to meet, say, pressing urban and welfare problems. We already have most of the knowledge and technology necessary, and where deficiencies exist, they can be overcome as work programs progress. Our real need is to *organize* the available resources better and *apply* them more effectively. The experience gained in NASA can surely help to that end.

In making these statements, I am not seeking, as some may contend, new assignments for NASA or added work for the aerospace industry. I am not suggesting that those of us who have engaged in the aeronautics and space programs should be entrusted with other great tasks. My thought instead is that NASA's experiences—its failures as well as its successes—can help in the critically needed development of a proven way to organize and administer many large and complex enterprises. Because these enterprises require enormous investments of human and material resources, and concentrate great power in the hands of a few individuals, the costs of failures and abuses can be immense. Society needs as much assurance of success as it can have when it commits its resources to such enterprises.

Can Public Trust Be Justified?

A great complication in the work of large complex enterprises is that they deal with problems which are often so complex that the average citizen cannot understand them. Donald Price, in his recent book entitled *The Scientific Estate*, underscores the seriousness of this situation. He writes:

"The industrial revolution brought its complexities, and relied heavily on new forms of expertise, but it did not challenge the assumption that the owner or manager, even without scientific knowledge, was able to control the policies of a business. And the same general belief was fundamental to our governmental system: the key ideas, if not the lesser details, could be understood by the legislature and debated before the public, and thus controlled by a chain of public responsibility. In one sense this was never true. . . . But it is much less apparently true today than it was, and a great many more people doubt it. The great issues of life and death, many people fear, are now so technically abstruse that they must be decided in secret by the few who have the ability to understand scientific complexities. We were already worrying about the alleged predominance of the executive over the legislature; now we worry lest even our elected executives cannot really understand what they are doing, lest they are only a facade that conceals the power of the scientists—many of whom are not even full-time officials, but have a primary loyalty to some university or corporation—who really control the decisions. . . . Science has thus given our political evolution a reverse twist. It has brought us back to a set of political problems that we thought we had disposed of forever by simple Constitutional principles." [6]

6. Donald K. Price, *The Scientific Estate* (Cambridge, Mass., The Belknap Press of Harvard University Press, 1957), p. 15 ff.

These are sobering considerations. Some might say that they logically lead to the conclusion that our democratic system must be modified, that it must give way to some kind of absolutist setup, perhaps some sort of technocracy. I take a different view. I believe that the kind of adaptive organization previously described offers a proven, low-risk answer to the problem. The public may not be able to comprehend all the nuances of the enterprise or see clearly what all their consequences will be. But its trust and confidence can be earned if the enterprise operates in the open and subject to public scrutiny, and if its leaders report regularly, in detail, and in understandable terms whether or not it is accomplishing what it was set up to do. I believe management should regularly include in its reports evaluations of whether the accomplishments seem to be worth what they are costing—doing this when the public wants to know and not just when the leaders themselves wish to report.

Some other policies that will help win public confidence will be discussed later in this chapter, using NASA as a case example. To appreciate the significance of these policies, let us first review the demands and pressures on NASA which have had to be taken into account by its leaders. This review should dispel any notion that NASA's task has been easier or simpler than that faced by public leaders in other areas of national concern.

Demands and Pressures

No single endeavor in U.S. history has equaled the NASA aeronautical and space programs in complexity. Few have involved so many unknowns and uncertainties, or have been so dependent for success on the "mysteries" of science and advanced technology. Few have presented as wide a range of problems in organization and management. And fewer still have held such popular interest, been subject to such public examination, and required such a unique degree of faith and trust on the part of the public. Seven characteristics have distinguished these programs.

First, *NASA has been assigned multiple objectives.* To begin with, there was the need for speed in restoring the technological-strategic balance that had been upset by the USSR in 1957 with its Sputnik. NASA was expected "to do something now" to offset the advantage the Soviets had gained. Related to this was the more far-reaching and fundamental objective of developing the basic capabilities necessary for the United States to reach up through the earth's atmosphere and to become a spacefaring nation second to none, to attain preeminence in space.

Then there was a variety of particular assignments, all interrelated but each of importance in itself: (a) to study the space environment by scientific instruments involving the use of sounding rockets, earth satellites, and deep space probes; (b) to begin the exploration of space by man himself; (c) to search for extraterrestrial life and thus find out whether we are alone in this vast universe; (d) to apply space science and technology for peaceful purposes to promote human welfare; and (e) to expand space science and technology as a basis for assuring national defense and welfare.

Second, *the programs have required working at the frontiers of knowledge and technology and have involved the construction of facilities and equipment, much of them without precedent.* For much of its life, NASA has found itself facing problems for which no solution was available. It has had to rely upon men and women with special, often unique skills, with high intelligence and creativity—individuals who by their very nature raise difficult problems of organization and management. Experts from the whole range of disciplines, from astronomy through zoology, have been required. Most tasks have needed more than a multidisciplinary effort; in effect, a fusing

126

of disciplines has been needed. New kinds of facilities have had to be provided, running all the way from the two million square foot Michoud booster assembly facility to vacuum chambers, centrifuges, and other machines to stimulate the hard vacuum and other extreme conditions of outer space. These varying, unique, and interrelated requirements for personnel and new kinds of facilities have greatly complicated the tasks of organization and management. $3 billion were invested in new facilities to add to the $1 billion investment that had been made prior to 1961.

Third, *long lead times have been required.* These lead times, coupled with uncertainties and rapidly evolving technologies, have added many complexities to the task of organizing the effort. A span of years is often required from the conception of a new space mission until the launch vehicle, the payload, and attendant facilities are designed, built, tested, launched, and the resulting data returned. Meanwhile, some early assumptions will have been revised, or new knowledge or technology will have generated substantial alteration.

This characteristic of space missions places a major premium on realism in planning and replanning and on grouping and regrouping of resources. It also means that a substantial period will always exist between public investments and visible major payoffs. This fact complicates the difficulties of securing continuing support.

Fourth, *a high order of reliability has been an absolute necessity.* Cost, public concern over each mission, and the risks to human life have combined to create a demand for a degree of reliability seldom required in other fields. The imaginative concepts of scientists and engineers, and the unique equipment which they have developed, have necessitated a wide use of simulation techniques. The ability to simulate complex environments and their interrelationships to complex machines and instruments has been developed almost to the level of a science.

The use of simulation and testing now assures a high degree

of reliability, but this must be obtained within much tighter time schedules than has historically been the case in complex research and development undertakings. Also, of course, there is little room for trial and error.

Fifth, under the provisions established for NASA operations, *space missions have been carried on under the persistent and exacting scrutiny of the mass media, the public, the Congress, the scientific community, and friends and foes at home and abroad.* Space missions, which are the final test of much of our work, have been and will almost certainly continue to be front page news. Those engaged in these tasks work in a goldfish bowl and are expected to interpret, explain, and defend in detail what they are doing and why they are doing it. Obviously, this policy adds to the time pressures of men and women who are already under great pressure, but it helps importantly to solve the problems of public confidence and accountability which were described earlier. As I pointed out recently, "A decision to do a large complex job cannot be simply reached 'at the top' and then carried through. . . . The basic decisions . . . are made by votes . . . Votes determine whether an endeavor is to be started . . . whether it is to continue . . . and for what changing or developing purposes. The voting process is integral to the operation itself." [7]

Sixth, *aeronautical and space programs have been peculiarly and intricately interrelated with the state of public sentiment or concern—the political environment or mood.* A significant change in this environment—the Soviet breakthrough with Sputnik—sparked the initiation of the program. Such developments as a new political situation (e.g., that in 1961), the ups and downs in international activities, shifting views as to Soviet intentions and purposes, Congressional and popular reaction to an accident in the space program (e.g., the Apollo fire of January 1967), and popular concern over the outbreak of

7. *Space Age Management* (New York, McGraw-Hill Book Company, Inc., 1969), p. 89.

a riot, place on NASA a critically important need for flexibility in organizational structure and management processes in order to adjust to new situations and demands. NASA's programs have always been peculiarly dependent on assurance that a continuing "critical mass" of support will exist. As with an airplane, these programs must have initial support adequate to attain the equivalent of "flying speed," and sufficient support must continue to maintain the airplane's equivalent of an efficient flight pattern.

NASA's space programs, in turn, have had and will continue to have an important impact on public sentiment. Some effects have been direct and immediate, as when measurements made by spacecraft reach the scientific community, or contracts modify the economic and employment situation in a city or state, or the stimulation of technological innovation changes practices in industry, medicine, communications, weather services, or transportation. Other effects are secondary and tertiary in nature and tend to alter attitudes, as when millions of people acquire new concepts of motion, or time, or the place of man in the vastness of space.

Seventh is the *crucial role that feedback and quick response to feedback signals have had to play in every phase of planning and operation.* For NASA, as for other complex endeavors conducted in a turbulent environment, a high degree of disequilibrium is essential if the maneuverability necessary to maintain control is to be maintained. Yet the forces of disequilibrium must not be too great; they must at all times be within management's power to influence, so that it can maneuver and respond. This means that management needs sufficient advance warning of unexpected difficulties, incipient failures, or emerging opportunities. The signals of trouble or opportunity must be in a form that those responsible for control can recognize and respond to. Enormous amounts of information have to be generated, *but information* alone is not enough. Means have to be devised and employed to sift from

129

a mass of disparate data the facts that are needed at any given moment, and to deliver them at that moment to the critical point of decision.

While the foregoing characteristics have distinguished the NASA programs from routine endeavors, they can hardly be considered unique. Similar characteristics are likely to be possessed by other tasks of unusual complexity requiring concentration of large and diverse human and material resources and involving the use of new knowledge and advanced technology. Moreover until we bring ourselves to anticipate and act upon difficult problems in advance of crises, performance of these tasks will require working under conditions of great stress and strain.

Avoidance of Crash Approach

Now let us turn to some of the basic policy questions which arise when an organization starts operating under conditions like those just described. One of the first questions is inevitably that of speed, pace, and deadlines. Granted that the leaders are determined to go "all out," how ambitious a timetable should they set?

In the case of NASA, during the first years work had to proceed against a background of great impatience on the part of many people and their elected representatives. At the same time, the agency was being organized from components of government agencies already in existence, and it was instituting large new programs (and carrying forward older programs) to increase our national capability in aeronautics and space.

The easiest course we could have followed would have been to put the program on a crash basis. There was ample precedent for such an approach, and the spirit of the country was certainly tolerant—one might even say demanding—of this. We could have aggregated personnel and other resources in a giant monolithic organization, scoured the country for scientists and engineers to incorporate into the organization, built massive new government installations, created our own construction units to build the test and launch facilities, and so on. We could have demanded that the entire program be put on the highest priority basis, and we could have commandeered elements of key industries. We could have focused our energies and resources on the achievement in the shortest possible time of a number of space spectaculars that would "take the heat off" ourselves and the nation.

However, we did *not* adopt this course. While we wanted to get moving toward space preeminence as quickly as feasible, we also wanted to build soundly and for the long term as well as the short. We wanted not simply to get into space, but to achieve a well-rounded and lasting capability that would enable us to do the wide variety of things that we knew would soon become possible. Above all, we wanted the country and its institutions to be the stronger and not the weaker because of the space program. In short, we decided against winning the race at any cost. This was our approach in the early days, and it has been followed ever since.

It may be of value to leaders in other endeavors to note that NASA has had the benefit of a farsighted legislative base. The National Aeronautics and Space Act of 1958 is in many ways an outstanding legislative achievement. It followed intensive studies and consultations within and outside the government on all aspects of the space question, as well as of what we had done in the past to meet similar situations. It recognized that technology would have to precede science for success in many space endeavors. It also recognized that both general and security needs could be served by developments in space, and it provided for a division of labor between civilian agencies and the Department of Defense. It carried forward the concepts of the atoms-for-peace program, but it did not require that work to go forward through an international organization. It called

131

for operations in the open and for the inclusion of the scientific community in the planning, conduct, and reporting of work.

On the administrative side, the Act returned to the principle established in the Constitution of reliance on a single executive rather than on a board, commission, or council. At the same time, it freed the agency of some of the restraints of existing Civil Service regulations. And it avoided any hard and fast provisions regarding choice of missions, organizational structure, and operational procedures, thus leaving the way open for NASA and its executives to be as adaptive as the situation from time to time might require.

I should also point out that within the Congress many of the ablest and most experienced and influential of its members were deeply concerned with the space program and its success. In many years of government experience I have learned that no factor can contribute more to the success of an undertaking than for its elements to have the trust, confidence, and support of wise and strong leaders in Congress. That NASA enjoyed such support also greatly contributed to its ability to follow an adaptive course.

Choice of Objectives

As the history of planning great projects shows, the choice of principal objectives is a crucial one. In this regard, there is a valuable lesson to be learned from NASA's experience.

The organization committed itself to a lunar landing by 1970. In retrospect, this objective seems deceptively obvious. At the time, however, it was not at all obvious. I have already mentioned the multiplicity of objectives that were set and the range of disparate tasks that were assigned to NASA in early 1961. I have also noted the diversity of organizational elements that went to make up NASA; no other new agency in the history of the Executive Branch of the Federal Government has been created through the transfer of so many units from other departments and agencies. These agencies were already engaged in a large number of ongoing developmental programs and projects, each with its special purposes and its special supporting theories and concepts, as well as its special vested interests. As might be expected, therefore, many differing schools of thought existed as to what would best serve our nation's needs in space, and there were strong-willed and influential champions of each of those schools. How could such diverse views be pulled together?

We decided to set for ourselves a number of missions, including, of course, the Apollo lunar mission, that were sufficiently challenging, and sufficiently complex and difficult in scientific, technological, and administrative requirements as to furnish in total a balanced science and technology development program. In effect, we established a focal point around which could be organized, in a purposeful and coordinated way, a *range* of activities that would give us both the general and the specific capabilities needed for the attainment of national pre-eminence.

Dr. Hugh Dryden, who served as Deputy Administrator of NASA from its establishment in 1958 until his death in December 1965, summarized in June 1961 the considerations that underlay our Apollo decision. He wrote:

"The setting of the difficult goal of landing a man on the moon and a return to earth has the highly important role of accelerating the development of space science and technology, motivating the scientists and engineers who are engaged in this effort to move forward with urgency, and integrating their efforts in a way that cannot be accomplished by a disconnected series of research investigations in the several fields. It is important to realize, however, that the real values and purposes are not in the mere accomplishment of man setting foot on the moon, but rather in the great cooperative national effort in the development of science and technology which is stimulated by this goal. . . . The national enterprise involved in

133

the goal of manned lunar landing and return within the decade is an activity of critical impact on the future of this nation as an industrial and military power, and as a leader of a free world." [8]

Now, I do not mean to suggest that something similar to a "moon goal" is needed or will work for other large and complex undertakings. I do believe, however, that for success in such undertakings the same sort of *approach* that we followed and which resulted in selection of the moon goal is necessary. I believe, more specifically, that it is necessary to make the most careful analysis of all known needs at the start, to fix on a goal or set of goals that will encompass all these needs, and at the same time to make adequate allowances for unknown factors and unexpected developments. While it is necessary to establish an organizational and operational plan that will enable the carrying out of diverse activities directed to purposefully correlated ends, it is also necessary to ensure that adjustments to reality can be made when conditions turn out differently from those anticipated.

What is the implication of this principle for planning to solve the problems of our urban centers? To save our cities, we need to meet transportation needs, housing needs, human relations needs, health needs, educational and employability needs, and waste disposal needs, among others; we need to deal with air and water pollution problems, crime control, and so on down the well-known list. But to attack each of these problems individually, as we seem intent on doing, is not likely to meet the total need. We must view the individual projects and their possible solutions as interdependent elements in a single whole, and adopt an integrated approach in organizing ourselves to deal with them. Such an approach is not easy; it presents stupendous difficulties. Yet I believe that for our cities, as for space exploration, an integrated attack will prove vastly more effective than any "individual components" approach.

8. Hugh L. Dryden in a letter to U.S. Senator Robert S. Kerr, June 22, 1961.

Drawing on Other Organizations

When a large new enterprise is created to meet a need in an area where other agencies and departments have already been working, the question of organizational relationships is bound to arise. How is the new enterprise to relate itself to other organizations in the field? This issue has political consequences as well as implications for mobilizing personnel and technological resources. The manner of dealing with it is likely to have a far-reaching impact on the future of the enterprise. At least, this was the case with NASA.

Prior to NASA's establishment, activities related to space research and development were carried on in a number of government departments and agencies. These activities were quite productive, surprisingly so in a number of instances. Nevertheless, and understandably, once the full impact of Sputnik was felt, the nation became impatient with the results of these uncoordinated efforts. And, as seems to be more or less customary under such circumstances, an entirely new agency—NASA—was brought into being to get a critical job done.

Under its legislative charter, and particularly after the 1961 decision for a greatly expanded and accelerated space effort, NASA could have proceeded with the buildup of a large and highly centralized department-like structure. This would have been the more or less normal thing to do, and, as noted earlier, it would have been the easiest from a strictly administrative standpoint. But the NASA program was considered too complex to bring together in a single organization all or even most of the expertise needed. We *could* have tried this, but instead we adopted the policy of utilizing existing organizations and institutions as much as we could. This operated to spread our problems over the largest number of able minds and to draw upon the range of the nation's scientific and industrial competence in the locations where it existed. This approach also helped nurture "grass roots" cooperation and support of NASA.

135

The policy was applied in the first instance to the laboratories, research and development centers, and other installations transferred to NASA from other government agencies. These establishments were left in place and allowed a large degree of operational and administrative autonomy. They were delegated contractual authority up to $5 million, subject to central review.

Where NASA has found it necessary to add to its in-house capabilities, it has done so not by expanding its central headquarters in Washington, but by strengthening and adding to the regional centers. Employment in Washington has never exceeded 2,500. This contrasts with a peak of some 33,000 in the regional establishments and a total work force of 420,000.

NASA has also made extensive use of the manpower and facilities available in other government agencies. We have, for example, turned to the U.S. Army Corps of Engineers to manage our construction programs, which required, at their peak, a work force of 40,000 men and women, and represent a capital investment of $3 billion. We have similarly relied on other specialized units of the Department of Defense, the Bureau of Standards, the Weather Bureau, and many other organizations for much of our research and development. We have been assisted on many problems by the National Science Foundation. And we have borrowed from the Armed Services and from other agencies many of those people who have manned and directed our various projects.

A major NASA policy has been to rely on contracts with nongovernmental establishments and institutions for the work they were qualified to do. In fact, over 99% of all funds invested in the NASA program have been spent outside the government. (In some years this amount has reached 95%.) Principal reliance has, of course, been placed on industry, but we have also drawn heavily on universities (200 of them, altogether), and such private organizations as the National Academy of Sciences, the National Academy of Engineering, the National Academy of Public Administration, and a long list of others.

Staying on Top of the Job

The spreading of NASA's work load over a large number of institutions and agencies raises an important question: Can management effectively control work done outside the organization and see that standards, deadlines, and so forth are met?

The answer is "Yes" so long as the organization itself has enough in-house capability—scientific, managerial, and engineering—to plan, administer, watch over, and assist the research and development work being done by others. It is not possible to rely upon even the most complex contracting system where accountants and lawyers are primarily responsible for performance. In NASA we have found that we must be able to speak and understand the language of those on whom we rely, to know as much about the problems they are dealing with as they do, to check and supplement their work in our own laboratories, to step in when required with the necessary specialists, and, in some cases, help untangle snarled situations.

In other words, we have to learn to be active participants in all phases of the projects that we entrust to others—but without undermining their discipline and control. The latter qualification is important. Our society cannot afford the creation of one massive organization after another to cope with every new, complex situation that arises. We cannot continue the practice of "government by crisis." We must develop and systematize methods and procedures whereby we can combine, dismantle, and recombine elements of existing establishments in and outside of government to get big and increasingly complex jobs done. We must learn how to marshal and use the great resources available in our established organizations in response to shift-

137

ing needs and goals. This deployment must be accomplished without disruption of those organizations and institutions or diminution of their ability to perform the *other* tasks with which they are concerned.

Strengthening the Partners

This brings me to a particularly important feature of NASA's approach. As we have used industry, universities, and other institutions to carry the main burden of the work program, we have as a matter of deliberate policy done so in a way to strengthen rather than weaken those institutions.

With respect to industry, we have been willing to pay a fair price, including a fair profit, for work done. This is essential in areas where large research-and-development efforts will not lead to large follow-up orders for production work. We have employed incentive contracts. We have encouraged and stimulated the utilization by industry of the latest technology. We have assisted in developing new capabilities within existing enterprises.

For universites, we have taken many steps that encourage research on the campus, rather than tempt the researcher to leave the campus. This has aided teaching and graduate training. We have provided doctoral training support for several thousand scientists and engineers. We have assisted in the construction on the campus of new laboratories and other research and training facilities. We have done all we could to encourage improvements in both curriculum and program and to stimulate the melding of discipline so as to increase the capabilities of universities and their graduates to deal with modern day problems. We have endeavored to help universities become "trusted sources of knowledge" in our society.

In so doing, we have not limited ourselves to a few great universities. We have also worked closely with less well-known

138

universities when these could demonstrate merit or promise of merit.

Our overall aim has been to effect a mutually beneficial working partnership between the universities, industry, and the government. We have operated on the principle that there is no inherent quarrel between public and private purposes, but that there is instead a coincidence of interest which offers a sound basis for genuine teamwork to the benefit of both sides.

NASA has been concerned not alone with the prime effects of its work on society, but with second- and third-order impacts as well. I must acknowledge that our understanding of this matter of second- and third-order effects and how to control them to desired ends is as yet rudimentary. But we have learned enough to appreciate that closest attention must be paid to them, particularly as they relate to society's basic institutions and values.

Anticipating Changing Situations

When a large, complex organization is created to handle a long-term assignment, the one thing planners can be sure of is that conditions, pressures, and demands on the organization will change from time to time. The tempo of activity will change; so will the scale of operations. However, neither the timing nor the nature of the changes can be foreseen precisely. How are such uncertainties to be taken into account?

At the inception of the enlarged space effort in 1961, it was clear that the NASA assignment would be an evolving one. We saw the probability of four major stages: *first,* a period of rapid build-up of capabilities and facilities, during which maximal inputs of resources and manpower would be required; *second,* a period of leveling off, or maturing, during which emphasis would shift from the development of capabilities to the use of capabilities already created, and during which there would be

139

a decline of new inputs and resources and manpower; *third,* a period of transition preparatory to putting the space endeavor on a long haul or regularized basis; and *fourth,* a period, extending into the indefinite future, during which space explorations and activities would be carried on as a normal and more or less routine part of our national life.

We recognized that each of these stages would require essentially different organizational and administrative systems and procedures, and that it was important that we avoid freezing ourselves into any set pattern during any one stage, at least, until the final one of regularized activity. Consequently, we not only kept the NASA administrative structure flexible, but also made a practice of regularly restructuring it. Management has, as a matter of fact, used structural reorganization as an important administrative device and as a means of exercising overall leadership.

We also recognized that in a project-type endeavor, acceleration would have to be followed by deceleration and that many operations involving both governmental and non-governmental manpower and facilities would have only a limited usefulness. We accepted the need to end these operations after their purposes were met. In other words, we foresaw that the NASA program would involve areas of declining activity as well as areas where newly approved projects were building up. By 1968, NASA had already reduced the scale of its total activities to about one-half the peak level which was attained in 1965.

Preparing for Political Change

An organization like NASA is likely to live through several changes of administration. Since such changes affect the organization in a variety of ways, steps should be taken to prepare for them.

As the election of 1968 approached, Dr. Thomas Paine, the

Deputy Administrator, and I made two commitments to President Lyndon B. Johnson. Dr. Paine promised to remain as Deputy Administrator under any president or administration for at least a year after the change of administration, if he was wanted; he stated that he would be as ready to leave as he would be to stay. My own commitment (having announced my intention to retire as head of NASA) was not to take any job involving compensation outside the U.S. Government before January 20, 1969, and to be available to Dr. Paine on at least a half-time consulting basis, in an office down the hall, on any matter on which he wished to consult me.

I told Dr. Paine and the President that I intended to use the other half of my time on the government-wide problems of transition from President Johnson to his successor. These problems have interested me for many years. My first acquaintance with them was in 1932, when I had just finished two years of duty as a U.S. Marine Corps reserve officer and joined the staff of the House Rules Committee. From that vantage point I saw Franklin D. Roosevelt elected, then experienced the four months hiatus before he was inaugurated. Inaugurations in those days took place in March, not in January, and the Rules Committee was a strategic and important place. In fact, its chairman, Edwin W. Pou, met with speaker John Garner and the party whip, Congressman McDuffy, every morning at ten o'clock, and they decided what the House would do that day. The House met at noon, did as instructed, and adjourned. In 1960 I was a member of the group set up by The Brookings Institution to work with the problems of transfer from President Dwight D. Eisenhower to President-elect John F. Kennedy. I wanted to follow the 1968–69 transition to add another increment of knowledge in this important area.

In preparing for leadership changes at NASA, beginning in the fall of 1967, we thought of a good many things. For instance, we decided if for some reason Dr. Paine should become incapacitated or lose his life in an airplane accident, I could

141

be appointed right away, by means of a recess appointment, to resume the Administrator's work. In such ways we attempted to relieve tension, to figure out what should and could be done without taking sides regarding individuals or parties. We wanted to tell the next President, in effect, "You can have anything you want in the way of NASA leadership. Here is the situation, wide open. Just remember you've got to fly five Saturn 5's next year."

Efforts in Other Countries

What about the advanced-technology programs of other countries? Japan has been making rapid progress on a variety of projects outside the area of basic science; the latter may be a problem for that country. As for the nations of Western Europe, they have suffered from inability to provide what we have provided quite well in the United States, that is, effective interaction between the engineers who are trying out things and scientists at the "cutting edge" of research. Only with such interaction can the engineer find the scientist who is out in front in a field and talk with him before committing himself to the final decisions that mean success or failure in his design. Nevertheless, Western Europe possesses a strong desire to see technology provide an avenue to new things, such as the communications satellites and other innovations that appear quite interesting from a commercial standpoint. Some nations are reaching for new solutions to the old problems; for example, France has made a recent reorganization of its university structure, and Germany is analyzing the role that should be played by the Max Planck Institute. And while there are a good many tensions between the different countries of Western Europe, by and large the scientific groups have a good base of support. The future might be much clearer but for the fact that, in the minds of the policymakers, finance ministers, and budget directors, the task of applying science to the development of markets and profits seems to be disconnected from basic research.

As for the USSR, I believe there is no doubt whatever that it has shown a very great capability to mobilize both science and technology, and to learn the basic scientific facts needed for engineers to produce working systems. The Soviets have built facilities both in aeronautics and in space which are capable of producing a large number of prototype developments. They are capable of putting these new developments into operation and finding out how they work. And they have the capability in many fields to choose a course of action intelligently after building prototypes, experimenting with them, and finding out how they work. Moreover, they can relate technological choices to their political objectives as a nation. They have other advantages, too. In the case of the supersonic transport, for instance, the Russians can fly that machine within the U.S.S.R. over a number of routes where they need not worry too much about sonic booms, and under conditions such that any accidents will not be played up in the press and on TV as they would be in the United States. Thus they can learn through experience how to move into world markets with the new transport.

Many observers and visitors to the Soviet Union agree that it will improve its competitive position significantly within a few years. Also noteworthy are the research and development concentrations the Soviets have been putting together. They seem to be grouping people and facilities, and bringing them into physical proximity with each other. I find this effort of theirs quite interesting.

Meeting the National Interest

No one thing, it seems to me, is as important in gaining acceptance of the use of large, complex endeavors and programs

143

as the demonstration of a capacity for the orderly phasing down of activities when that is appropriate. Organizations, private as well as public, have a way of generating dynamics to keep themselves going after they are not needed, or even to increase the scope of their activities.

This is perhaps one reason why Americans generally resist the initiation of special efforts to meet difficult problems until there is a full-blown crisis. And here, I believe, the instincts of our citizens are in part sound. We cannot afford to go on and on adding self-perpetuating organizations to our governmental structure. Of course, these is another side to the story: We also cannot afford to dismantle and scrap effective organizations that have been built up at great cost each time a special job is finished. We cannot afford this in particular when the organizations in question are capable of initiating and leading the new technological developments essential for the continued advancement of our society.

How is our nation to deal with this dilemma? We all need to give it much attention and study. Progress can be encouraged through a better understanding of what is needed for governmental elements to adapt effectively to changing conditions, and to reorganize and regroup components and units as problems, situations, and opportunities change. Such an ability to adapt will require important legislative changes as well as strong leadership in the Executive Branch. But first we must have more knowledge of what produces success or failure. NASA's experience is a valuable step in that direction.

Index

145

Ferry, Wilbur, 56
First National Bank of Boston, The, 21
Forbes magazine, 121–123
Ford, Henry, 48
Ford Motor Company, 63, 77
Foreman, George, 81
Fortune magazine, 34, 92
France, 142
French National Plan, 91
Fromm, Erich, 31–32

Galbraith, John Kenneth, 32, 57
Garner, John, 141
General Electric Company, 53
George Washington University, 63
Germany, 101–102, 142
Gevaert company, 92
Ghana, 105
Goethe, 13–14
Goldston, Eli, 21
Gray, Elisha, 53
Great Britain, 89–90, 91, 99, 101

Hahn, Loeser, Freedheim, Dean & Wellman, 21
Haloid Company, The, 45
Hamlet, 14
Harvard Business Review, 3
Harvard Business School, 28, 87
Harvard Law School, 3, 21
Harvard University, 3, 21
Heilbroner, Robert, 53
housing, 34–40
Housing and Urban Development, Department of, 36
Hughes Aircraft Company, 63

India, 23–24, 96, 102
Industrial Reorganisation Corporation, 92

industrial revolution, 50, 89–90, 124
International Business Machine Corporation, 28
International Center of New England, 21
invention, 13–14

Japan, 102, 142
Job Corps, 80–81
John Hancock Mutual Life Insurance Company, 21
Johnson, Lyndon B., 141
Johnson & Johnson, 30

Kennedy, John F., 33, 113, 141
Kerr, Robert S., 134 fn.

Lever Brothers, 96
Leverhulme, Lord, 95
Levinson, Harry, 28, 32
Lincoln Electric Company, 48
Lincoln, Joseph, 48
Litton Industries, Inc., 63, 66–67, 70–75, 78–81
London Graduate School of Business Studies, 87
Lunar Orbiter, 115

McDonnell, J. S., 113
McNamara, Robert, 33–34
McNeill, William H., 119–120
man, nature of, 10–11
management succession, 140–142
Mao Tse-Tung, 50
marketing, 56, 100–102
Massachusetts Institute of Technology, 3, 23

146

147

148